FIX-IT and FORGET-IT®
Family Vacation
COOKBOOK

FIX-IT and FORGET-IT®
Family Vacation
COOKBOOK

SLOW COOKER MEALS
FOR YOUR RV, BOAT, CABIN, OR BEACH HOUSE

HOPE COMERFORD

Good Books
New York, New York

Table of Contents

Welcome to *Fix-It and Forget-It Family Vacation Cookbook* ⚜ 1

Tips for Traveling with a Slow Cooker or Instant Pot from Hope and Friends ⚜ 1

Choosing a Slow Cooker ⚜ 3

Slow Cooking Tips and Tricks and Other Things You May Not Know ⚜ 7

Getting Started with Your Instant Pot ⚜ 8

Instant Pot Tips and Tricks and Other Things You May Not Know ⚜ 11

Breakfast ⚜ 15

Appetizers & Snacks ⚜ 43

Soups, Stews & Chilies ⚜ 61

Chicken ⚜ 63

Beef ⚜ 75

Pork ⚜ 91

Meatless ⚜ 101

Main Dishes ⚜ 111

Chicken ⚜ 113

Beef ⚜ 137

Pork ⚜ 163

Side Dishes & Vegetables ⚜ 183

Desserts & Beverages ⚜ 227

Desserts ⚜ 229

Beverages ⚜ 261

Metric Equivalent Measurements ⚜ 275

Recipe and Ingredient Index ⚜ 276

About the Author ⚜ 287

Welcome to *Fix-It and Forget-It Family Vacation Cookbook*

Just because you're on vacation doesn't mean you have to take a vacation from home-cooked meals! Whether you're traveling across the country in your RV, relaxing on your boat, making memories around a campfire, or spending time with family at the beach house, you can put your slow cookers and Instant Pots to good use for you! Whether you're having an evening of appetizers with those at campsites around you, want breakfast that's ready when you wake up, want dinner to cook while you're out adventuring, or are ready to warm up with a hot beverage or dessert, this book has it all! Don't forget to check out the section with tips for traveling with your slow cooker or Instant Pot so you're prepared and ready for this new cooking adventure!

Tips for Traveling with a Slow Cooker or Instant Pot from Hope and Friends

- Plan all your meals out ahead of time! Read each recipe carefully. Make a list of the things you'll need and prep as much as you can beforehand.
- Don't forget the utensils! Make sure to look at each recipe you plan to make and pack all the cooking tools you'll need to make each recipe and to serve it.
- If you're camping and won't have access to a stove top, brown ground beef, turkey, etc. ahead of time and bag it up. Be sure to label each bag for which recipe you'll need it.
- Buy pre-cut meats and veggies! Kitchen space may be really tight when traveling, so make things easier on yourself by purchasing them pre-cut.
- If you know you won't have the counter space to chop veggies, chop them all ahead of time. Bag them up or even vacuum seal them. Be sure to label them so you know which recipes they are for.
- Put all the spices and seasonings needed in a ziplock bag labeled for which meal you need them. This way you don't have to drag all of the containers with you. Works great for sauces, meatloaf, stews, etc.
  —*Brenda Schnarrs, Clinton Township, MI*
- Assemble your meals in freezer bags ahead of time and label them. Keep them in a cooler and pull them out when you're ready to cook.
  —*Kim Hayden, Clinton Township, MI*

- Pre-cook your slow cooker meals, freeze them, then warm them up in the slow cooker when camping. This way, 1) you don't have to pack a bunch of individual ingredients, 2) the frozen meals act as additional ice packs in your coolers when traveling to keep other items you might need cold, and 3) it saves on prep/cooking time so you can spend time doing your other fun camping activities!

  —Melissa Belardi-Hodges, Troy, MI

- Use disposable liners for your crock for easy clean-up!

  —Jennifer Sharer, Clinton Township, MI

- Check to make sure your wiring is good to handle the current.

  —Jacob Stine, Farmington Hills, MI

- Bring extension cords and power strips just in case you need them!

- If you're in an RV, make sure yours can handle the power of the appliance you're bringing.

- Call ahead at your campground to make sure they have outlets for you to plug in your slow cooker or Instant Pot.

Choosing a Slow Cooker

Not all slow cookers are created equal . . . or work equally well for everyone!

Those of us who use slow cookers frequently know we have our own preferences when it comes to which slow cooker we choose to use. For instance, I love my programmable slow cooker, but there are many programmable slow cookers I've tried that I've strongly disliked. Why? Because some go by increments of 15 or 30 minutes and some go by 4, 6, 8, or 10 hours. I dislike those restrictions, but I have family and friends who don't mind them at all! I am also pretty brand loyal when it comes to my manual slow cookers because I've had great success with those and have had unsuccessful moments with slow cookers of other brands. So, which slow cooker(s) is/are best for your household?

It really depends on how many people you're feeding and if you're gone for long periods of time. Here are my recommendations:

For 2–3 person household	3–5-quart slow cooker
For 4–5 person household	5–6-quart slow cooker
For a 6+ person household	6½–7-quart slow cooker

Large slow cooker advantages/disadvantages:

Advantages:

- You can fit a loaf pan or a baking dish into a 6- or 7-quart, depending on the shape of your cooker. That allows you to make bread or cakes, or even smaller quantities of main dishes. (Take your favorite baking dish and loaf pan along when you shop for a cooker to make sure they'll fit inside.)
- You can feed large groups of people, or make larger quantities of food, allowing for leftovers, or meals, to freeze.

Disadvantages:

- They take up more storage room.
- They don't fit as neatly into a dishwasher.
- If your crock isn't ⅔–¾ full, you may burn your food.

Small slow cooker advantages/disadvantages:

Advantages:
- They're great for lots of appetizers, for serving hot drinks, for baking cakes straight in the crock, and for dorm rooms or apartments.
- Great option for making recipes of smaller quantities.

Disadvantages:
- Food in smaller quantities tends to cook more quickly than larger amounts. So keep an eye on it.
- Chances are, you won't have many leftovers. So, if you like to have leftovers, a smaller slow cooker may not be a good option for you.

My recommendation:

Have at least two slow cookers: one around 3 to 4 quarts and one 6 quarts or larger. A third would be a huge bonus (and a great advantage to your cooking repertoire!). The advantage of having at least a couple is you can make a larger variety of recipes. Also, you can make at least two or three dishes at once for a whole meal.

Manual vs. Programmable

If you are gone for only six to eight hours a day, a manual slow cooker might be just fine for you. If you are gone for more than eight hours during the day, I would highly recommend purchasing a programmable slow cooker that will switch to warm when the cook time you set is up. It will allow you to cook a wider variety of recipes.

The two I use most frequently are my 4-quart manual slow cooker and my 6½-quart programmable slow cooker. I like that I can make smaller portions in my 4-quart slow cooker on days I don't need or want leftovers, but I also love how my 6½-quart slow cooker can accommodate whole chickens, turkey breasts, hams, or big batches of soups. I use them both often.

Get to know your slow cooker . . .

Plan a little time to get acquainted with your slow cooker. Each slow cooker has its own personality—just like your oven (and your car). Plus, many new slow cookers cook hotter and faster than earlier models. I think that with all of the concern for food safety, the slow cooker manufacturers have amped up their settings so that "High," "Low," and "Warm" are all higher temperatures than in the older models. That means they cook hotter—and therefore, faster—

than the first slow cookers. The beauty of these little machines is that they're supposed to cook low and slow. We count on that when we flip the switch in the morning before we leave the house for ten hours or so. So, because none of us knows what kind of temperament our slow cooker has until we try it out, nor how hot it cooks—don't assume anything. Save yourself a disappointment and make the first recipe in your new slow cooker on a day when you're at home. Cook it for the shortest amount of time the recipe calls for. Then, check the food to see if it's done. Or if you start smelling food that seems to be finished, turn off the cooker and rescue your food.

Also, all slow cookers seem to have a "hot spot," which is of great importance to know, especially when baking with your slow cooker. This spot may tend to burn food in that area if you're not careful. If you're baking directly in your slow cooker, I recommend covering the "hot spot" with some foil.

Take notes . . .

Don't be afraid to make notes in your cookbook. It's yours! Chances are, it will eventually get passed down to someone in your family and they will love and appreciate all of your musings. Take note of which slow cooker you used and exactly how long it took to cook the recipe. The next time you make it, you won't need to try to remember. Apply what you learned to the next recipes you make in your cooker. If another recipe says it needs to cook 7–9 hours, and you've discovered your slow cooker cooks on the faster side, cook that recipe for 6–6½ hours and then check it. You can always cook a recipe longer—but you can't reverse things if it's overdone.

Get creative . . .

If you know your morning is going to be hectic, prepare everything the night before, take the crock out so it warms up to room temperature when you first get up in the morning, then plug it in and turn it on as you're leaving the house.

If you want to make something that has a short cook time and you're going to be gone longer than that, cook it the night before and refrigerate it for the next day. Warm it up when you get home. Or, cook those recipes on the weekend when you know you'll be home and eat them later in the week.

Slow Cooking Tips and Tricks and Other Things You May Not Know

- Slow cookers tend to work best when they're ⅔ to ¾ of the way full. You may need to increase the cooking time if you've exceeded that amount, or reduce it if you've put in less than that. If you're going to exceed that limit, it would be best to reduce the recipe, or split it between two slow cookers. (Remember how I suggested owning at least two or three slow cookers?)

- Keep your veggies on the bottom. That puts them in more direct contact with the heat. The fuller your slow cooker, the longer it will take its contents to cook. Also, the more densely packed the cooker's contents are, the longer they will take to cook. And finally, the larger the chunks of meat or vegetables, the more time they will need to cook.

- Keep the lid on! Every time you take a peek, you lose 20 minutes of cooking time. Please take this into consideration each time you lift the lid! I know, some of you can't help yourself and are going to lift anyway. Just don't forget to tack on 20 minutes to your cook time for each time you peeked!

- Sometimes it's beneficial to remove the lid. If you'd like your dish to thicken a bit, take the lid off during the last half hour to hour of cooking time.

- If you have a big slow cooker (7- to 8-quart), you can cook a small batch in it by putting the recipe ingredients into an oven-safe baking dish or baking pan and then placing that into the cooker's crock. First, put a trivet or some metal jar rings on the bottom of the crock, and then set your dish or pan on top of them. Or a loaf pan may "hook onto" the top ridges of the crock belonging to a large oval cooker and hang there straight and securely, "baking" a cake or quick bread. Cover the cooker and flip it on.

- The outside of your slow cooker will be hot! Please remember to keep it out of reach of children and keep that in mind for yourself as well!

- Get yourself a quick-read meat thermometer and use it! This helps remove the question of whether or not your meat is fully cooked, and helps prevent you from overcooking your meat as well.

Internal Cooking Temperatures:
- Beef—125–130°F (rare); 140–145°F (medium); 160°F (well-done)
- Pork—140–145°F (rare); 145–150°F (medium); 160°F (well-done)
- Turkey and Chicken—165°F
- Frozen meat: The basic rule of thumb is, don't put frozen meat into the slow cooker. The meat does not reach the proper internal temperature in time. This especially applies to thick cuts of meat! Proceed with caution!

- Add fresh herbs 10 minutes before the end of the cooking time to maximize their flavor.
- If your recipe calls for cooked pasta, add it 10 minutes before the end of the cooking time if the cooker is on High; 30 minutes before the end of the cooking time if it's on Low. Then the pasta won't get mushy.
- If your recipe calls for sour cream or cream, stir it in 5 minutes before the end of the cooking time. You want it to heat but not boil or simmer.

Approximate Slow Cooker Temperatures (Remember, each slow cooker is different):
- High—212°F–300°F
- Low—170°F–200°F
- Simmer—185°F
- Warm—165°F

Cooked and dried bean measurements:
- 16-oz. can, drained = about 1¾ cups beans
- 19-oz. can, drained = about 2 cups beans
- 1 lb. dried beans (about 2½ cups) = 5 cups cooked beans

Getting Started with Your Instant Pot

Get to know your Instant Pot . . .

The very first thing most Instant Pot owners do is called the water test. It helps you get to know your Instant Pot a bit, familiarizes you with it, and might even take a bit of your apprehension away (because if you're anything like me, I was scared to death to use it!).

Step 1: Plug in your Instant Pot. This may seem obvious to some, but when we're nervous about using a new appliance, sometimes we forget things like this.

Step 2: Make sure the inner pot is inserted in the cooker. You should NEVER attempt to cook anything in your device without the inner pot, or you will ruin your Instant Pot. Food should never come into contact with the actual housing unit.

Step 3: The inner pot has lines for each cup (how convenient, right?!). Fill the inner pot with water until it reaches the 3-cup line.

Step 4: Check the sealing ring to be sure it's secure and in place. You should not be able to move it around. If it's not in place properly, you may experience issues with the pot letting out a lot of steam while cooking, or not coming to pressure.

Step 5: Seal the lid. There is an arrow on the lid between and "open" and "close." There is also an arrow on the top of the base of the Instant Pot between a picture of a locked lock and an unlocked lock. Line those arrows up, then turn the lid toward the picture of the lock (left). You will hear a noise that will indicate the lid is locked. If you do not hear a noise, it's not locked. Try it again.

Step 6: ALWAYS check to see if the steam valve on top of the lid is turned to "sealing." If it's not on "sealing" and is on "venting," it will not be able to come to pressure.

Step 7: Press the "Steam" button and use the +/- arrow to set it to 2 minutes. Once it's at the desired time, you don't need to press anything else. In a few seconds, the Instant Pot will begin all on its own. Those of us with digital slow cookers have a tendency to look for the "start" button, but there isn't one on the Instant Pot.

Step 8: Now you wait for the "magic" to happen! The "cooking" will begin once the device comes to pressure. This can take anywhere from 5–30 minutes, as I've found in my experience. Then, you will see the countdown happen (from the time you set it). After that, the Instant Pot will beep, which means your meal is done!

Step 9: Your Instant Pot will now automatically switch to "warm" and begin a count of how many minutes it's been on warm. The next part is where you either wait for the NPR, or natural pressure release (meaning the pressure releases all on its own) or you do what's called a QR, or quick release (meaning, you manually release the pressure). Which method you choose depends on what you're cooking, but in this case, you can choose either since it's just water. For NPR, you will wait for the lever to move all the way back over to "venting" and watch the pinion (float valve) next to the lever. It will be flush with the lid when at full pressure and will drop when the pressure is done releasing. If you choose QR, be very careful not to have your hands over the vent as the steam is very hot and you can burn yourself.

The Three Most Important Buttons You Need to Know About . . .

You will find the majority of recipes will use the following three buttons:

Manual/Pressure Cook: Some older models tend to say "Manual" and the newer models seem to say "Pressure Cook." They mean the same thing. From here, you use the +/- button to change the cook time. After several seconds, the Instant Pot will begin its process.

Sauté: Many recipes will have you sauté vegetables or brown meat before beginning the pressure cooking process. For this setting, you will not use the lid of the Instant Pot.

Keep Warm/Cancel: This may just be the most important button on the Instant Pot. When you forget to use the +/- buttons to change the time for a recipe, or you press a wrong button, you can hit "keep warm/cancel" and it will turn your Instant Pot off for you.

What Do All the Buttons Do?

With so many buttons, it's hard to remember what each one does or means. You can use this as a quick guide in a pinch.

Soup/Broth. This button cooks at high pressure for 30 minutes. It can be adjusted using the +/- buttons to cook more for 40 minutes, or less for 20 minutes.

Meat/Stew. This button cooks at high pressure for 35 minutes. It can be adjusted using the +/- buttons to cook more for 45 minutes, or less for 20 minutes.

Bean/Chili. This button cooks at high pressure for 30 minutes. It can be adjusted using the +/- buttons to cook more for 40 minutes, or less for 25 minutes.

Poultry. This button cooks at high pressure for 15 minutes. It can be adjusted using the +/- buttons to cook more for 30 minutes, or less for 5 minutes.

Rice. This button cooks at low pressure and is the only fully automatic program. It is for cooking white rice and will automatically adjust the cooking time depending on the amount of water and rice in the cooking pot.

Multigrain. This button cooks at high pressure for 40 minutes. It can be adjusted using the +/- buttons to cook more for 45 minutes of warm water soaking time and 60 minutes pressure cooking time, or less for 20 minutes.

Porridge. This button cooks at high pressure for 20 minutes. It can be adjusted using the +/- buttons to cook more for 30 minutes, or less for 15 minutes.

Steam. This button cooks at high pressure for 10 minutes. It can be adjusted using the +/- buttons to cook more for 15 minutes, or less for 3 minutes. Always use a rack or steamer basket with this function because it heats at full power continuously while it's coming to pressure and you do not want food in direct contact with the bottom of the pressure cooking pot or it will burn. Once it reaches pressure, the steam button regulates pressure by cycling on and off, similar to the other pressure buttons.

Less | Normal | More. Adjust between the *Less | Normal | More* settings by pressing the same cooking function button repeatedly until you get to the desired setting. (Older versions use the *Adjust* button.)

+/- Buttons. Adjust the cook time up [+] or down [-]. (On newer models, you can also press and hold [-] or [+] for 3 seconds to turn sound OFF or ON.)

Cake. This button cooks at high pressure for 30 minutes. It can be adjusted using the +/- buttons to cook more for 40 minutes, or less for 25 minutes.

Egg. This button cooks at high pressure for 5 minutes. It can be adjusted using the +/- buttons to cook more for 6 minutes, or less for 4 minutes.

Instant Pot Tips and Tricks and Other Things You May Not Know

- Never attempt to cook directly in the Instant Pot without the Inner Pot!

- Once you set the time, you can walk away. It will show the time you set it to, then will change to the word "on" while the pressure builds. Once the Instant Pot has come to pressure, you will once again see the time you set it for. It will count down from there.

- Always make sure your sealing ring is securely in place. If it shows signs of wear or tear, it needs to be replaced.

- Have a sealing ring for savory recipes and a separate sealing ring for sweet recipes. Many people report their desserts tasting like a roast (or another savory food) if they try to use the same sealing ring for all recipes.

- The stainless steel rack (trivet) that your Instant Pot comes with can be used to keep food from being completely submerged in liquid, like baking potatoes or ground beef. It can also be used to set another pot on, for pot-in-pot cooking.

- If you use warm or hot liquid instead of cold liquid, you may need to adjust the cooking time or your food may not come out done.

- Always double-check to see that the valve on the lid is set to "sealing" and not "venting" when you first lock the lid. This will save you from your Instant Pot not coming to pressure.

- Use Natural Pressure Release for tougher cuts of meat, recipes with high starch (like rice or grains), and recipes with a high volume of liquid. This means you let the Instant Pot naturally release pressure. The little bobbin will fall once pressure is released completely.

- Use Quick Release for more delicate cuts of meat and vegetables, like seafood, chicken breasts, and steaming vegetables. This means you manually turn the vent (being careful not to put your hand over the vent!) to release the pressure. The little bobbin will fall once pressure is released completely.

- Make sure there is a clear pathway for the steam to release. The last thing you want is to ruin the bottom of your cupboards with all that steam.

- You MUST use liquid in your Instant Pot. The MINIMUM amount of liquid you should have in your inner pot is ½ cup—however, most recipes work best with at least 1 cup.

- Do NOT overfill your Instant Pot! It should only be half full for rice or beans (food that expands greatly when cooked) or two-thirds of the way full for most everything else. Do not fill it to the max filled line.

- In this book, the Cooking Time DOES NOT take into account the amount of time it will take your Instant Pot to come to pressure, or the amount of time it will take the Instant Pot to release pressure. Be aware of this when choosing a recipe to make.
- If your Instant Pot is not coming to pressure, it's usually because the sealing ring is not on properly, or the vent is not set to "sealing."
- The more liquid, or the colder the ingredients, the longer it will take for the Instant Pot to come to pressure.
- Always make sure that the Instant Pot is dry before inserting the inner pot, and make sure the inner pot is dry before inserting it into the Instant Pot.
- Doubling a recipe does not change the cook time, but instead it will take longer to come up to pressure.
- You do not always need to double the liquid when doubling a recipe. Depending on what you're making, more liquid may make your food too watery. Use your best judgment.

Slow Cooker	Instant Pot
Warm	Less or Low
Low	Normal or Medium
High	High

Breakfast

Layered Breakfast Casserole

Cathy Boshart
Lebanon, PA

Makes 8–10 servings
Prep. Time: 30 minutes   ✿   Cooling Time: 4–8 hours
✿   Cooking Time: 1 hour   ✿   Ideal slow-cooker size: 6-qt.

6 cups shredded potatoes
2 dozen eggs, scrambled
1 lb. chopped ham
12 oz. Velveeta cheese, shredded

1. Spread the shredded potatoes in bottom of greased slow cooker.

2. Spoon the scrambled eggs over top of potatoes.

3. Layer ham evenly over eggs. Sprinkle with cheese.

4. Cover and cook on Low for 1 hour or until cheese is melted.

Tips:

1. This is a perfect dish to serve on a buffet.

2. You can prepare through the first instruction in Step 3 a day ahead (chill in the fridge overnight), but sprinkle the cheese over top just before cooking. If you've refrigerated the slow cooker overnight, allow it to reach room temperature before turning it on and reheating the dish.

3. Serve with toasted English muffins and fresh fruit.

Variation:

You can make half, or even one fourth, of this recipe if this quantity is too large. And you don't need to scramble the eggs before placing them in the cooker. Simply mix the cooked potatoes, ham, and cheese together in the slow cooker. Beat the eggs in a separate bowl, along with salt and pepper to taste. Then pour them over the other ingredients and cook on Low for 2–4 hours.

—Kendra Dreps, Liberty, PA

Breakfast Bake

Kristi See
Weskan, KS

Makes 10 servings
Prep. Time: 15 minutes ✤ Cooking Time: 3–4 hours ✤ Ideal slow-cooker size: 4- to 5-qt.

12 eggs
1½–2 cups grated cheese, your choice
1 cup diced cooked ham
1 cup milk
1 tsp. salt
½ tsp. pepper

1. Beat eggs. Pour into slow cooker.

2. Mix in remaining ingredients.

3. Cover and cook on Low 3–4 hours.

Breakfast Sausage Casserole

Kendra Dreps
Liberty, PA

Makes 8 servings
Prep. Time: 15 minutes ♣ Chilling Time: 8 hours ♣ Cooking Time: 4 hours ♣ Ideal slow-cooker size: 3-qt.

6 eggs
2 cups milk
8 slices bread, cubed
2 cups shredded cheddar cheese
1 lb. loose sausage, browned and drained

1. Mix together eggs and milk in a large bowl.

2. Stir in bread cubes, cheese, and sausage.

3. Place in greased slow cooker.

4. Refrigerate overnight.

5. Cook on Low 4 hours.

Variation:

Use cubed cooked ham instead of sausage.

Easy Egg and Sausage Puff

Sara Kinsinger
Stuarts Draft, VA

Makes 6 servings
Prep. Time: 10–15 minutes   *Cooking Time: 2–2½ hours*   *Ideal slow-cooker size: 2- to 4-qt.*

1 lb. loose sausage, browned and drained

6 eggs

1 cup all-purpose baking mix

1 cup shredded cheddar cheese

2 cups milk

¼ tsp. dry mustard, *optional*

1. Spray the interior of slow cooker with nonstick cooking spray.

2. Mix all ingredients in slow cooker.

3. Cover and cook on High 1 hour. Turn to Low and cook 1–1½ hours, or until the dish is fully cooked in the center.

Huevos Rancheros in Crock

Pat Bishop
Bedminster, PA

Makes 6 servings
Prep. Time: 25 minutes ☘ *Cooking Time: 2 hours* ☘ *Ideal slow-cooker size: 6-qt.*

3 cups gluten-free salsa, room temperature

2 cups cooked beans, drained, room temperature

6 eggs, room temperature

salt and pepper to taste

⅓ cup reduced-fat grated Mexican blend cheese, *optional*

1. Mix salsa and beans in the slow cooker.

2. Cook on High for 1 hour or until steaming.

3. With a spoon, make 6 evenly spaced dents in the salsa mixture; try not to expose the bottom of the crock. Break an egg into each dent.

4. Salt and pepper eggs. Sprinkle with cheese if you wish.

5. Cover and continue to cook on High until egg whites are set and yolks are as firm as you like them, approximately 20–40 minutes.

6. To serve, scoop out an egg with some beans and salsa.

Serving Suggestion:

Serve with warm white corn tortillas.

Easy Spinach Quiche

Sue Hamilton
Minooka, IL

Makes 6 servings
Prep. Time: 15 minutes ⚘ Cooking Time: 3 hours ⚘ Ideal slow-cooker size: 4- to 5-qt. oval

2 pkgs. flat refrigerated pie dough

5 eggs

I cup spinach dip

4 oz. prosciutto, diced

4 oz. pepper jack cheese, diced

1. Press pie crusts into cold slow cooker. Overlap seams by ¼ inch, pressing to seal. Tear off pieces to fit up the sides, pressing pieces together at seams.

2. Cover. Cook on High 1½ hours.

3. Beat eggs in a mixing bowl. Stir in spinach dip, prosciutto, and cheese. Pour into hot crust.

4. Cover. Cook on High 1½ hours, or until filling is set.

5. Let stand 5 minutes before serving.

Poached Eggs

Instant Pot

Hope Comerford
Clinton Township, MI

Makes 6–8 servings
Prep. Time: 5 minutes ❧ Cooking Time: 2–5 minutes ❧ Setting: Steam
Pressure: High ❧ Release: Manual

1 cup water

4 large eggs

1. Place the trivet in the bottom of the inner pot of the Instant Pot and pour in the water.

2. You will need small silicone egg poacher cups that will fit in your Instant Pot to hold the eggs. Spray each silicone cup with nonstick cooking spray.

3. Crack each egg and pour it into the prepared cup.

4. Very carefully place the silicone cups into the Inner Pot so they do not spill.

5. Secure the lid by locking it into place and turn the vent to the sealing position.

6. Push the Steam button and adjust the time— 2 minutes for a very runny egg all the way to 5 minutes for a slightly runny egg.

7. When the timer beeps, release the pressure manually and remove the lid, being very careful not to let the condensation in the lid drip into your eggs.

8. Very carefully remove the silicone cups from the inner pot.

9. Carefully remove the poached eggs from each silicone cup and serve immediately.

Quick and Easy Instant Pot Cinnamon Rolls

Hope Comerford
Clinton Township, MI

Makes 5 servings
Prep. Time: 5 minutes & Cooking Time: 13 minutes & Setting: Manual
Pressure: High & Release: Manual

2 cups water

17½-oz. can Pillsbury Grands! Original Cinnamon Rolls with Icing

1. Place the 2 cups water in the inner pot of the Instant Pot, then place the trivet inside.

2. Cover the trivet with aluminum foil so that it also kind of wraps up the sides.

3. Grease a 7-inch round pan and arrange the cinnamon rolls inside. Set the icing aside. Place this pan on top of the aluminum foil inside the inner pot.

4. Secure the lid and make sure vent is on sealing. Press Manual, high pressure for 13 minutes.

5. Release the pressure manually when cooking time is up.

6. Remove the lid carefully so that the moisture does not drip on the cinnamon rolls.

7. Drizzle the icing on top of the cinnamon rolls and serve.

Streusel Cake

Jean Butzer
Batavia, NY

Makes 8–10 servings
Prep. Time: 10 minutes ⚹ Cooking Time: 3–4 hours ⚹ Ideal slow-cooker size: 3-qt.

16-oz. pkg. pound cake mix, batter prepared according to package directions

¼ cup packed brown sugar

1 Tbsp. flour

¼ cup chopped nuts

1 tsp. cinnamon

1. Liberally grease and flour a 2-lb. coffee can, or slow-cooker baking insert, that fits into your slow cooker. Pour prepared cake mix into coffee can or baking insert.

2. In a small bowl, mix brown sugar, flour, nuts, and cinnamon together. Sprinkle over top of cake mix.

3. Place coffee tin or baking insert in slow cooker. Cover top of tin or insert with several layers of paper towels.

4. Cover cooker itself and cook on High 3–4 hours, or until toothpick inserted in center of cake comes out clean.

5. Remove baking tin from slow cooker and allow to cool for 30 minutes before cutting into wedges to serve.

Tip:

Make sure you have all the ingredients for the cake mix before you take this one on the road, or prepare the cake mix ahead of time according to box directions, then store the batter in a ziplock bag and label it for this recipe.

Blueberry Fancy

Leticia A. Zehr
Lowville, NY

Makes 12 servings
Prep. Time: 10–15 minutes ⚬ Cooking Time: 3–4 hours ⚬ Ideal slow-cooker size: 5-qt.

1 loaf Italian bread, cubed, *divided*
1 pint blueberries, *divided*
8 oz. cream cheese, cubed, *divided*
6 eggs
1½ cups milk

1. Place half the bread cubes in the slow cooker.

2. Drop half the blueberries over top the bread.

3. Sprinkle half the cream cheese cubes over the blueberries.

4. Repeat all 3 layers.

5. In a mixing bowl, whisk together eggs and milk. Pour over all ingredients.

6. Cover and cook on Low until the dish is custardy and set.

Serving Suggestion:

Serve with maple syrup or blueberry sauce.

Variation:

Add 1 tsp. vanilla extract to Step 5.

Apple Breakfast Cobbler

Anona M. Teel
Bangor, PA

Makes 8 servings
Prep. time: 25 minutes ⚬ *Cooking Time: 2–9 hours* ⚬ *Ideal slow-cooker size: 4- or 5-qt.*

8 medium apples, cored, peeled, sliced
2 Tbsp. maple syrup
dash of cinnamon
juice of 1 lemon
2 Tbsp. coconut oil, melted
2 cups granola

1. Combine ingredients in the slow cooker.

2. Cover. Cook on Low 7–9 hours (while you sleep!), or on High 2–3 hours (after you're up in the morning).

Breakfast Apples

Joyce Bowman
Lady Lake, FL

Jeanette Oberholtzer
Manheim, PA

Makes 4 servings
Prep. Time: 10–15 minutes ❦ *Cooking Time: 2–8 hours* ❦ *Ideal slow-cooker size: 3-qt.*

4 medium-sized apples, peeled and sliced

¼ cup honey

1 tsp. cinnamon

2 Tbsp. melted coconut oil

2 cups dry granola cereal

1. Place apples in your slow cooker.

2. Combine remaining ingredients. Sprinkle the mixture evenly over the apples.

3. Cover and cook on Low 6–8 hours, or overnight, or on High 2–3 hours.

Serving suggestion:
Serve as a side dish to bacon and bagels, or use as a topping for waffles, French toast, pancakes, or cooked oatmeal.

Breakfast Oatmeal

Donna Conto
Saylorsburg, PA

Makes 6 servings
Prep. Time: 5 minutes ☙ *Cooking Time: 8 hours* ☙ *Ideal slow-cooker size: 4-qt.*

2 cups dry rolled oats

4 cups water

1 tsp. salt

½–1 cup chopped dates, or raisins, or cranberries, or a mixture of any of these fruits

1. Combine all ingredients in slow cooker.

2. Cover and cook on Low overnight, or for 8 hours.

Overnight Oatmeal

Jody Moore
Pendleton, IN

Makes 4–5 servings
Prep. Time: 5 minutes   ☙   Cooking Time: 8 hours   ☙   Ideal slow-cooker size: 3-qt.

1 cup steel cut oats
4 cups water

1. Combine ingredients in the slow cooker.

2. Cover and cook on Low overnight, or for 8 hours.

3. Stir before serving.

Tip:
Please note that steel cut oats are called for. They are different—with more texture, requiring a longer cooking time—than old-fashioned or rolled oatmeal.

Serving suggestion:
Serve with brown sugar, ground cinnamon, fruit preserves, jam, jelly, pumpkin pie spice, fresh fruit, maple syrup, or your other favorite toppings.

German Chocolate Oatmeal

Hope Comerford
Clinton Township, MI

Makes 4 servings
Prep. Time: 5 minutes ⚖ *Cooking Time: 6–8 hours* ⚖ *Ideal slow-cooker size: 3-qt.*

2 cups steel cut oats

8 cups unsweetened coconut milk

¼ cup unsweetened cocoa powder

¼ tsp. kosher salt

brown sugar, *optional*

sweetened shredded coconut (enough for a sprinkle on top of each bowl)

1. Spray crock with nonstick spray.

2. Place steel cut oats, coconut milk, cocoa powder, and salt into crock and stir to mix.

3. Cover and cook on Low for 6–8 hours.

4. To serve, top each bowl of oatmeal with desired amount of brown sugar, if desired, and a sprinkle of shredded coconut.

Appetizers & Snacks

Insta Popcorn

Instant Pot

Hope Comerford
Clinton Township, MI

Makes 5–6 servings
Prep. Time: 1 minute ⚭ *Cooking Time: about 5 minutes* ⚭ *Setting: Sauté*

2 Tbsp. coconut oil

½ cup popcorn kernels

sea salt to taste

1. Set the Instant Pot to Sauté.

2. Melt the coconut oil in the inner pot, then add the popcorn kernels and stir.

3. Press Adjust to bring the temperature up to high.

4. When the corn starts popping, secure the lid on the Instant Pot.

5. When you no longer hear popping, turn off the Instant Pot, remove the lid, and pour the popcorn into a bowl.

6. Season the popcorn with sea salt to your liking.

Chili Nuts

Barbara Aston
Ashdown, AR

Makes 5 cups nuts
Prep. Time: 5 minutes ❧ Cooking Time: 2–2½ hours ❧ Ideal slow-cooker size: 3-qt.

¼ cup melted butter

2 (12-oz.) cans cocktail peanuts

1⅝-oz. pkg. chili seasoning mix

1. Pour butter over nuts in slow cooker. Sprinkle in dry chili mix. Toss together.

2. Cover. Heat on Low 2–2½ hours. Turn to High. Remove lid and cook 10–15 minutes.

Serving suggestion:
Serve warm or cool.

Sweet 'n Sour Meatballs

Valerie Drobel
Carlisle, PA

Sharon Hannaby
Frederick, MD

Makes 15–20 servings
Prep. Time: 10 minutes ❧ Cooking Time: 2–4 hours ❧ Ideal slow-cooker size: 3- to 4-qt.

12-oz. jar grape jelly

12-oz. jar chili sauce

2 (1-lb.) bags prepared frozen
meatballs, thawed

1. Combine jelly and sauce in slow cooker. Stir well.

2. Add meatballs. Stir to coat.

3. Cover and heat on Low 4 hours, or on High 2 hours. Keep slow cooker on Low while serving.

Variation:

Instead of meatballs, use 2 (1-lb.) packages smoked cocktail sausages.

—Krista Hershberger, Elverson, PA

Barbecued Cocktail Sausages

Jena Hammond
Traverse City, MI

Makes 48–60 appetizer servings
Prep. Time: 5 minutes ⚶ *Cooking Time: 4 hours* ⚶ *Ideal slow-cooker size: 4-qt.*

4 (16-oz.) pkgs. little smoked cocktail sausages

18-oz. bottle barbecue sauce

1. Mix ingredients together in slow cooker.

2. Cover and cook on Low for 4 hours.

Chili Cheese Dip

Vicki Dinkel
Sharon Springs, KS

Makes 8 servings
Prep. Time: 10–15 minutes ⚘ *Cooking Time: 4 hours* ⚘ *Ideal slow-cooker size: 2-qt.*

1 onion, diced

8-oz. pkg. fat-free cream cheese, cubed

2 (15-oz.) cans low-fat vegetarian chili without beans

2 tsp. garlic salt

1½ cups salsa

Baked tortilla chips, for serving

1. If you have access to a stove top, lightly brown onions in skillet sprayed with nonfat cooking spray and transfer them to the crock; otherwise, place the diced onions un-browned in the crock.

2. Stir in cream cheese, chili, garlic salt, and salsa.

3. Cover. Cook on Low 4 hours, stirring occasionally.

4. Serve with baked tortilla chips.

Southwest Hot Chip Dip

Annabelle Unternahrer
Shipshewana, IN

Makes 15–20 servings
Prep. Time: 15 minutes   ❧   Cooking Time: 1½–4 hours   ❧   Ideal slow-cooker size: 3-qt.

1 lb. ground beef, browned, crumbled fine, and drained

2 (15-oz.) cans refried beans

2 (10-oz.) cans diced tomatoes and chilies

1 pkg. taco seasoning

1 lb. Velveeta cheese, cubed

1. Combine ground beef, beans, tomatoes, and taco seasoning in slow cooker.

2. Cover. Cook on Low 3–4 hours, or on High 1½ hours.

3. Add cheese. Stir occasionally. Heat until cheese is melted.

Serving Suggestion:

Serve with tortilla chips. This can be a main dish when served alongside a soup.

Chili-Cheese Taco Dip

Kim Stoltzfus
New Holland, PA

Makes 10–12 servings
Prep. Time: 15 minutes ♣ Cooking Time: 1–1½ hours ♣ Ideal slow-cooker size: 1- to 1½-qt.

1 lb. ground beef, browned and drained

1 (15-oz.) can chili, without beans

1 lb. mild Mexican Velveeta cheese, cubed

1. Combine beef, chili, and cheese in slow cooker.

2. Cover. Cook on Low 1–1½ hours, or until cheese is melted, stirring occasionally to blend ingredients.

Serving suggestion:

Serve warm with taco or tortilla chips.

Tina's Cheese Dip

Tina Houk
Clinton, MO

Makes 12 servings
Prep. Time: 5–10 minutes ⚬ Cooking Time: 1–1½ hours ⚬ Ideal slow-cooker size: 4-qt.

2 (8-oz.) pkgs. cream cheese, softened

3 (15½-oz.) cans chili

2 cups shredded cheddar or mozzarella cheese

1. Spread cream cheese in bottom of slow cooker.

2. Spread chili on top of cream cheese.

3. Top with shredded cheese.

4. Cover. Cook on Low 1–1½ hours, until shredded cheese is melted. Stir.

Serving suggestion:
Serve with tortilla chips.

Texas Queso Dip

Donna Treloar
Muncie, IN

Janie Steele
Moore, OK

Makes 2 qts. dip
Prep. Time: 10 minutes ❧ *Cooking Time: 2 hours* ❧ *Ideal slow-cooker size: 4-qt.*

2-lb. block mild Mexican Velveeta cheese, cubed

10-oz. can diced tomatoes with chilies

½ cup milk

1 lb. spicy ground pork sausage, browned and drained

1. Combine cheese, tomatoes, and milk in slow cooker.

2. Stir in browned sausage.

3. Cover and cook 2 hours on Low.

Serving suggestion:
Serve with tortilla chips.

Soups, Stews & Chilies

Chicken

Tasty Chicken Soup

Rhonda Freed
Lowville, NY

Makes 12 servings
Prep. Time: 10–15 minutes & Cooking Time: 6–7 hours & Ideal slow-cooker size: 4-qt.

12 cups chicken broth

2 cups chicken, cooked and cut into small pieces

1 cup shredded carrots

1 small onion

3 whole cloves

16-oz. bag of dry noodles, cooked, *optional*

1. Place broth, chicken, and carrots in slow cooker.

2. Peel onion. Using a toothpick, poke 3 holes on the cut ends. Carefully press cloves into 3 of the holes until only their round part shows. Add to slow cooker.

3. Cover and cook on High 6–7 hours.

4. If you'd like a thicker soup, add a bag of cooked fine egg noodles before serving.

Chunky Chicken Vegetable Soup

Janice Muller
Derwood, MD

Makes 6 servings
Prep. Time: 20 minutes ⚜ *Cooking Time: 2–6 hours* ⚜ *Ideal slow-cooker size: 3½- to 4-qt.*

2½ cups water

8-oz. can tomato sauce

10-oz. pkg. frozen mixed vegetables, partially thawed

1½ tsp. Italian seasoning

1 envelope dry chicken noodle soup mix

2 cups cut-up cooked chicken or turkey

1. Combine all ingredients in slow cooker.

2. Cook on Low 2–6 hours, depending upon how crunchy you like your vegetables.

Mary's Chicken and Rice Soup

Becky Frey
Lebanon, PA

Makes 8–10 servings
Prep. Time: 10–20 minutes ⚜ *Cooking Time: 3–4 hours* ⚜ *Ideal slow-cooker size: 3½-qt.*

4.4-oz. pkg. chicken-flavored rice and
sauce

2 cups diced, cooked chicken

15-oz. can diced tomatoes and green
chilies

49½-oz. can chicken broth

1. Place all ingredients in slow cooker. Stir until well mixed.

2. Cover and cook on Low 3–4 hours.

Serving suggestion:

Serve over corn chips and sprinkle with shredded cheese, if you wish.

Tip:

If you can't find tomatoes with chilies, add a can of plain diced tomatoes along with a 4-oz. can of diced green chiles. Or add the can of chilies anyway for extra heat.

Quick Taco Chicken Soup

Karen Waggoner
Joplin, MO

Makes 4–6 servings
Prep. Time: 5 minutes ⚬ Cooking Time: 1 hour ⚬ Ideal slow-cooker size: 4-qt.

12-oz. can cooked chicken, undrained
14-oz. can chicken broth
16-oz. jar mild thick-and-chunky salsa
15-oz. can ranch-style beans
15-oz. can whole-kernel corn

1. Mix all ingredients in slow cooker.

2. Cover and cook on High 1 hour. Keep warm on Low until ready to serve.

Easy Chicken Tortilla Soup

Becky Harder
Monument, CO

Makes 6–8 servings

Prep. Time: 5–10 minutes   ♣   Cooking Time: 8 hours   ♣   Ideal slow-cooker size: 4- to 5-qt.

4 chicken breast halves

2 (15-oz.) cans black beans, undrained

2 (15-oz.) cans Mexican stewed tomatoes, or Ro*Tel tomatoes

1 cup salsa (mild, medium, or hot, whichever you prefer)

4-oz. can chopped green chiles

14½-oz. can tomato sauce

tortilla chips

1. Combine all ingredients except tortilla chips in large slow cooker.

2. Cover. Cook on Low 8 hours.

3. Just before serving, remove chicken breasts and slice into bite-sized pieces. Stir into soup.

4. Put a handful of tortilla chips in each individual soup bowl. Ladle soup over chips.

Serving suggestion:

Top with shredded cheese.

Buffalo Chicken Wing Soup

Mary Lynn Miller
Reinholds, PA

Donna Neiter
Wausau, WI

Joette Droz
Kalona, IA

Makes 8 servings
Prep. Time: 10 minutes ❧ *Cooking Time: 4–5 hours* ❧ *Ideal slow-cooker size: 3-qt.*

6 cups milk

3 (10¾-oz.) cans condensed cream of chicken soup, undiluted

3 cups (about 1 lb.) shredded or cubed cooked chicken

1 cup (8 oz.) sour cream

1–8 Tbsp. hot pepper sauce, according to your preference for heat!

1. Combine milk and soup in slow cooker until smooth.

2. Stir in chicken.

3. Cover and cook on Low 3¾–4¾ hours.

4. Fifteen minutes before serving, stir in sour cream and hot sauce.

5. Cover and continue cooking just until bubbly.

Tip:

Start with a small amount of hot sauce, and then add more to suit your—and your diners'—tastes!

Turkey Chili

Dawn Day
Westminster, CA

Makes 6–8 servings
Prep. Time: 10–15 minutes ⚘ *Cooking Time: 8–9 hours* ⚘ *Ideal slow-cooker size: 3½- to 4-qt.*

1 large onion, chopped
2–3 Tbsp. oil
1 lb. ground turkey, browned
½ tsp. salt
3 Tbsp. chili powder
6-oz. can tomato paste
3 (1-lb.) cans small red beans, with liquid
1 cup frozen corn

1. If you have access to a stove top, sauté the onion in the oil, then place it in the crock. If you do not have access to a stove top, leave the chopped onion raw, place it in the crock, and omit the oil.

2. Combine all remaining ingredients in slow cooker. Mix well.

3. Cover. Cook on Low 8–9 hours.

Note from the cook:
Ground beef can be used in place of turkey.

Serving suggestion:
Serve over rice, topped with shredded cheddar cheese and sour cream.

Beef

Taco Soup

Norma Grieser
Clarksville, MI

Makes 4–6 servings
Prep. Time: 10–12 minutes   ❧   Cooking Time: 4–6 hours   ❧   Ideal slow-cooker size: 3-qt.

1 lb. ground beef, browned and drained
1 qt. tomato juice
15-oz. can kidney beans
1 envelope dry taco seasoning
10½-oz. can tomato soup
1 medium-sized onion, chopped, *optional*

1. Add all ingredients to slow cooker and stir until well combined.

2. Cover and cook on Low 4–6 hours.

Serving suggestion:
Serve with Doritos, sour cream, and shredded cheddar cheese as toppings, if you wish.

Variation:
Instead of tomato juice and tomato soup, substitute a 14½-oz. can stewed tomatoes and an 8-oz. can tomato sauce.

—Sharon Shank, Bridgewater, VA

Taco Soup with Pinto Beans

Janie Steele
Moore, OK

Makes 10–12 servings
Prep. Time: 15 minutes ⚘ *Cooking Time: 4 hours* ⚘ *Ideal slow-cooker size: 6½-qt.*

1 lb. ground beef, browned and drained
1 large onion, chopped
3 (14-oz.) cans pinto beans
14-oz. can tomatoes with chilies
14½-oz. can chopped tomatoes
15-oz. can tomato sauce
1 pkg. dry Hidden Valley Ranch Dressing mix
1 pkg. dry taco seasoning
15¼-oz. can corn, drained

1. Combine all ingredients in slow cooker.

2. Cover. Cook on Low 4 hours, or until ingredients are heated through.

Chili Taco Soup

Frances L. Kruba
Dundalk, MD

Makes 8 servings

Prep. Time: 25–30 minutes · *Cooking Time: 5–7 hours* · *Ideal slow-cooker size: 1- to 2-qt.*

2 lbs. lean stew meat, browned if you have access to a stove top
2 (15-oz.) cans stewed tomatoes, Mexican or regular
1 envelope dry taco seasoning mix
2 (15-oz.) cans pinto beans
15-oz. can whole-kernel corn
¾ cup water

1. Combine all ingredients in slow cooker.
2. Cover and cook on Low 5–7 hours.

Santa Fe Soup with Melted Cheese

Carla Koslowsky
Hillsboro, KS

Makes 8 servings
Prep. Time: 15 minutes ❧ *Cooking Time: 3 hours* ❧ *Ideal slow-cooker size: 4-qt.*

1 lb. Velveeta cheese, cubed
1 lb. ground beef, browned and drained
15¼-oz. can corn, undrained
15-oz. can kidney beans, undrained
14½-oz. can diced tomatoes with green chilies
14½-oz. can stewed tomatoes
2 Tbsp. dry taco seasoning

1. Combine all ingredients in slow cooker.

2. Cover. Cook on High 3 hours.

Serving suggestion:
Serve with corn chips as a side, or dip soft tortillas in individual servings in soup bowls.

Ground Beef Vegetable Soup

Renee Baum
Chambersburg, PA

Janet Oberholtzer
Ephrata, PA

Makes 10 servings
Prep. Time: 15 minutes   ❧   *Cooking Time: 8–9 hours*   ❧   *Ideal slow-cooker size: 5-qt.*

1 lb. ground beef, browned and drained

46-oz. can tomato, or V8, juice

16-oz. pkg. frozen mixed vegetables, thawed

2 cups frozen cubed hash browns, thawed

1 envelope dry onion soup mix

1. Combine all ingredients in the slow cooker.

2. Cover and cook on Low 8–9 hours, or until vegetables are cooked through.

Variations:

1. Instead of hash browns, use 2 cups cubed cooked potatoes.

   —Elsie Schlabach, Millersburg, OH

2. Instead of tomato or V8 juice, use 2 beef bouillon cubes dissolved in 2 cups boiling water. And instead of dry onion soup mix, use salt and pepper to taste.

   —Sharon Wantland, Menomonee Falls, WI

Beef Barley Soup

Stacie Skelly
Millersville, PA

Makes 8–10 servings
Prep. Time: 15 minutes & Cooking Time: 9¼–11½ hours & Ideal slow-cooker size: 6-qt.

3–4-lb. chuck roast

2 cups chopped carrots

6 cups vegetable, or tomato, juice, *divided*

2 cups quick-cook barley

water, to desired consistency

salt and pepper to taste, *optional*

1. Place roast, carrots, and 4 cups juice in slow cooker.

2. Cover and cook on Low 8–10 hours.

3. Remove roast. Place on platter and cover with foil to keep warm.

4. Meanwhile, add barley to slow cooker. Stir well. Turn heat to High and cook 45 minutes to 1 hour, until barley is tender.

5. While barley is cooking, cut meat into bite-sized pieces.

6. When barley is tender, return chopped beef to slow cooker. Add 2 cups juice, water if you wish, and salt and pepper, if you want. Cook for 30 minutes on High, or until soup is heated through.

Beef Stew

Leann Brown
Ronks, PA

Makes 6–8 servings
Prep. Time: 10–15 minutes ⚜ *Cooking Time: 5–6 hours* ⚜ *Ideal slow-cooker size: 5- to 6-qt.*

3 lbs. cubed beef

2 (12-oz.) jars beef gravy

2 cups chopped carrots

1 medium-sized onion, chopped

4 cups chopped potatoes

salt and pepper, *optional*

1. Place beef in slow cooker. Add remaining ingredients. Stir together well.

2. Cover and cook on Low 5–6 hours, or until meat and veggies are tender but not overcooked.

Lynn's Easy Stew

Veronica Sabo
Shelton, CT

Makes 5–6 servings
Prep. Time: 10 minutes ❧ Cooking Time: 5–8 hours ❧ Ideal slow-cooker size: 4- to 5-qt.

2 lbs. stew beef

4 ribs celery, cut into large pieces

3 cups carrots, cut up in large pieces

1 large onion, chopped

1 envelope dry onion soup mix

water

1. Place all ingredients in slow cooker. Stir together gently, but until well mixed. Add about 2 inches of water.

2. Cover and cook on High 5–8 hours, or until meat and vegetables are tender.

Extra Easy Chili

Jennifer Gehman
Harrisburg, PA

Makes 4–6 servings
Prep. Time: 10 minutes   ❧   Cooking Time: 4–8 hours   ❧   Ideal slow-cooker size: 4-qt.

I lb. ground beef or turkey, uncooked

I envelope dry chili seasoning mix

16-oz. can chili beans in sauce

2 (28-oz.) cans crushed or diced tomatoes seasoned with garlic and onion

1. Crumble meat in bottom of slow cooker.

2. Add remaining ingredients. Stir.

3. Cover. Cook on High 4–6 hours or Low 6–8 hours. Stir halfway through cooking time.

Serving suggestion:

Serve over white rice, topped with shredded cheddar cheese and chopped raw onions.

Chili with Two Beans

Patricia Fleischer
Carlisle, PA

Makes 6–8 servings
Prep. Time: 15 minutes ⚘ *Cooking Time: 4½–5 hours* ⚘ *Ideal slow-cooker size: 6-qt.*

I lb. ground beef, browned and drained

6-oz. can tomato paste

40½-oz. can kidney beans, undrained

2 (15½-oz.) cans pinto beans, undrained

2 Tbsp. chili powder

1. Combine all ingredients in slow cooker.

2. Cover and cook on Low 4½–5 hours.

Versatile Slow-Cooker Chili

Margaret H. Moffitt
Bartlett, TN

Makes 6–8 servings
Prep. Time: 25 minutes ⚭ Cooking Time: 6 hours ⚭ Ideal slow-cooker size: 3-qt.

1 lb. ground beef, or turkey, browned and drained

2 (15-oz.) cans tomato sauce

2 (15-oz.) cans kidney beans or black beans, drained

1 envelope dry chili seasoning

15-oz. can of water, or more or less

1. Combine all ingredients in the slow cooker.

2. Cover and cook on Low 6 hours.

Tip:

If you do not have time to brown your ground beef or turkey, just crumble it into your slow cooker without browning it. It will cook sufficiently during the 6 hours.

Pork

Kelly's Split Pea Soup

Kelly Evenson
Pittsboro, NC

Makes 8 servings
Prep. Time: 10 minutes ⚬ *Cooking Time: 8–9 hours* ⚬ *Ideal slow-cooker size: 4½-qt.*

2 cups dry split peas
2 qts. water
2 onions, chopped
2 carrots, peeled and sliced
4 slices Canadian bacon, chopped
2 Tbsp. chicken bouillon granules, or 2 chicken bouillon cubes
1 tsp. salt
¼–½ tsp. pepper

1. Combine all ingredients in slow cooker.

2. Cover. Cook on Low 8–9 hours.

Tip:

For a creamier soup, remove half of soup when done and purée. Stir back into rest of soup.

Mountain Bike Soup

Jonathan Gehman
Harrisonburg, VA

Makes 4 servings
Prep. Time: 10 minutes ⚜ *Cooking Time: 2–6 hours* ⚜ *Ideal slow-cooker size: 2- or 3-qt.*

12-oz. can chicken broth

12-oz. can V8 juice, regular or spicy

⅓ cup uncooked barley, rice, or broken spaghetti noodles

⅓ cup chopped pepperoni, ham, or bacon

15-oz. can cut green beans with liquid

1. Dump it all in your crock. Put on the lid. Turn it on Low.

2. Go for a long ride on your bike, from 2–6 hours.

Tip:

This soup seems to accept whatever vegetables you throw in: a little corn, okra, diced potatoes, shredded zucchini, whatever . . . I often add more liquid before serving if it seems to be getting more like stew and less like soup.

Smoked Sausage Stew

Carol Sherwood
Batavia, NY

Makes 4–5 servings
Prep. Time: 35–40 minutes ⚬ *Cooking Time: 4–5 hours* ⚬ *Ideal slow-cooker size: 5-qt.*

4–5 potatoes, peeled and cubed
2 (15-oz.) cans green beans
1 lb. smoked sausage, sliced
1 onion, chopped
2 Tbsp. butter

1. Layer potatoes, green beans, sausage, and onion in slow cooker in the order they are listed.

2. Dot top with butter.

3. Cook on Low 4–5 hours, or until potatoes are tender but not mushy.

Kielbasa Soup

Bernice M. Gnidovec
Streator, IL

Makes 8 servings
Prep. Time: 10 minutes ⚬ *Cooking Time: 12 hours* ⚬ *Ideal slow-cooker size: 8-qt.*

16-oz. pkg. frozen mixed vegetables, or your choice of vegetables

6-oz. can tomato paste

1 medium onion, chopped

3 medium potatoes, diced

1½ lbs. kielbasa, cut into ¼-inch pieces

4 qts. water

1. Combine all ingredients in large slow cooker.

2. Cover. Cook on Low 12 hours.

Ham and Bean Stew

Sharon Wantland
Menomonee Falls, WI

Makes 4–6 servings
Prep. Time: 15 minutes ⚬ *Cooking Time: 5–7 hours* ⚬ *Ideal slow-cooker size: 3-qt.*

2 (16-oz.) cans baked beans
2 medium potatoes, peeled and cubed
2 cups cubed ham
2 ribs celery, chopped
1 onion, chopped
½ cup water
1 Tbsp. cider vinegar
1 tsp. salt
⅛ tsp. pepper

1. Combine all ingredients in the slow cooker. Mix well.

2. Cover and cook on Low for 5–7 hours, or until the potatoes are tender.

Meatless

Harry's Vegetable Soup

Betty B. Dennison
Grove City, PA

Makes 16 servings
Prep. Time: 4–5 minutes ⚜ *Cooking Time: 2–4 hours* ⚜ *Ideal slow-cooker size: 4-qt.*

4 (15¼-oz.) cans mixed vegetables, drained

46-oz. can vegetable juice

4 cups beef broth

1 tsp. Mrs. Dash Original Blend

1. Mix all ingredients in a greased slow cooker.

2. Cover and cook on Low 4 hours or on High 2 hours.

Tomato Vegetable Soup

Elaine Sue Good
Tiskilwa, IL

Makes 8 servings
Prep. Time: 10 minutes   Cooking Time: 4–10 hours   Ideal slow-cooker size: 3½-qt.

2 cloves garlic, pressed and chopped

8- or 16-oz. pkg. frozen peppers and onions

3 Tbsp. Italian seasoning mix, or basil, oregano, etc.

32-oz. pkg. frozen mixed vegetables, or leftover vegetables, chopped

46-oz. can vegetable, or V8 juice, or Bloody Mary mix, or beef broth

1. Place pressed garlic cloves into bottom of slow cooker. Add peppers and onions.

2. Sprinkle seasonings over top.

3. Add vegetables. Then pour juice over all ingredients.

4. Cover and cook on High 4 hours, or on Low 8–10 hours.

6-Can Soup

Audrey L. Kneer
Williamsfield, IL

Makes 8 servings
Prep. Time: 10 minutes   ⚶   *Cooking Time: 3–4 hours*   ⚶   *Ideal slow-cooker size: 3½- or 4-qt.*

10¾-oz. can tomato soup
15-oz. can whole-kernel corn, drained
15-oz. can mixed vegetables, drained
15-oz. can chili beans, undrained
14½-oz. can diced tomatoes, undrained
14½-oz. can vegetable broth

1. Combine all ingredients in slow cooker.

2. Cover. Cook on Low 3–4 hours.

Broccoli Cheese Soup

Darla Sathre
Baxter, MN

Makes 8 servings
Prep. Time: 10 minutes ❧ *Cooking Time: 8–10 hours* ❧ *Ideal slow-cooker size: 4-qt.*

2 (16-oz.) pkgs. frozen chopped broccoli

2 (10¾-oz.) cans cheddar cheese soup

2 (12-oz.) cans evaporated milk

¼ cup finely chopped onions

½ tsp. seasoned salt

¼ tsp. pepper

1. Combine all ingredients in slow cooker.

2. Cover. Cook on Low 8–10 hours.

Cream of Broccoli Soup

Barb Yoder
Angola, IN

Makes 6–8 servings
Prep. Time: 10–15 minutes ❧ Cooking Time: 3–4 hours ❧ Ideal slow-cooker size: 4-qt.

1 small onion, chopped
20-oz. pkg. frozen broccoli
2 (10¾-oz.) cans cream of celery soup
10¾-oz. can cream of mushroom soup
1 cup grated American cheese
2 soup cans milk

1. Combine all ingredients in slow cooker.

2. Cover. Cook on Low 3–4 hours.

Beans and Tomato Chili

Becky Harder
Monument, CO

Makes 6–8 servings
Prep. Time: 5 minutes ⚬ Cooking Time: 4–8 hours ⚬ Ideal slow-cooker size: 4½-qt.

15-oz. can black beans, undrained

15-oz. can pinto beans, undrained

16-oz. can kidney beans, undrained

15-oz. can garbanzo beans, undrained

2 (14½-oz.) cans stewed tomatoes and juice

1 pkg. prepared chili seasoning

1. Pour beans, including their liquid, into slow cooker.

2. Stir in tomatoes and chili seasoning.

3. Cover. Cook on Low 4–8 hours.

Serving suggestion:
Serve with crackers, and top with grated cheddar cheese, sliced green onions, and sour cream, if desired.

Variation:
Add additional cans of white beans or 1 tsp. dried onion.

Main Dishes

Chicken

Slow Cooked Honey Garlic Chicken Thighs

Instant Pot

Colleen Heatwole
Burton, MI

Makes 2–4 servings

Prep. Time: 10 minutes ⚜ *Cooking Time: 4 hours* ⚜ *Setting: Slow Cook* ⚜ *Pressure: Low*

4 boneless, skinless chicken thighs

2 Tbsp. soy sauce

½ cup ketchup

⅓ cup honey

3 cloves garlic, minced

1 tsp. basil

1. Place chicken thighs in bottom of the inner pot of the Instant Pot.

2. Whisk remaining ingredients together in bowl and pour over chicken.

3. Cook covered on the Slow Cook function on low pressure for 4 hours. Check for doneness. If not tender, add additional time as needed.

Note from the cook:

Of course this can be done in conventional slow cooker as well.

Come-Back-for-More Barbecued Chicken

Leesa DeMartyn
Enola, PA

Makes 6–8 servings
Prep. Time: 10 minutes   ❧   Cooking Time: 6–8 hours   ❧   Ideal slow-cooker size: 5-qt.

6–8 chicken breast halves
1 cup ketchup
⅓ cup Worcestershire sauce
½ cup brown sugar
1 tsp. chili powder
½ cup water

1. Place chicken in slow cooker.

2. Whisk remaining ingredients in a large bowl. Pour sauce mixture over chicken.

3. Cover and cook on Low for 6–8 hours, or until chicken is tender but not overcooked.

Tip:

If the sauce begins to dry out as the dish cooks, stir in another ½ cup water.

Tender Barbecued Chicken

Mary Lynn Miller
Reinholds, PA

Makes 4–6 servings
Prep. Time: 10–15 minutes   ♣   Cooking Time: 8–10 hours   ♣   Ideal slow-cooker size: 5-qt.

3–4-lb. broiler/fryer chicken, cut up
1 medium-sized onion, thinly sliced
1 medium-sized lemon, thinly sliced
18-oz. bottle barbecue sauce
¾ cup cola

1. Place chicken in slow cooker. Top with onion and lemon slices.

2. Combine barbecue sauce and cola. Pour over all.

3. Cover and cook on Low 8–10 hours, or until chicken is tender but not dry.

Quickie Barbecued Chicken

Carol Sherwood
Batavia, NY

Sharon Shank
Bridgewater, VA

Makes 4 servings
Prep. Time: 20 minutes   ❧   Cooking Time: 3–7 hours   ❧   Ideal slow-cooker size: 4-qt.

4 boneless, skinless chicken breast halves

¾ cup chicken broth

1 cup barbecue sauce

1 medium-sized onion, sliced

salt to taste

pepper to taste

1. Place all ingredients in slow cooker. Stir gently.

2. Cook on High 3 hours, or on Low 6–7 hours, or until chicken is tender but not dry.

3. Serve the breast pieces whole, or cut up chicken and stir through the sauce.

Chicken Enchiladas

Jennifer Yoder Sommers
Harrisonburg, VA

Makes 4 servings
Prep. Time: 20 minutes ☘ Cooking Time: 4 hours ☘ Ideal slow-cooker size: 3-qt.

2 (10¾-oz.) cans cream of chicken or mushroom soup

4½-oz. can diced green chiles

2–3 boneless, skinless whole chicken breasts, cut into pieces

2 cups shredded cheddar cheese

5 (6-inch) flour tortillas

1. In a mixing bowl, combine soup, chiles, and chicken.

2. Spray the interior of the cooker with nonstick cooking spray.

3. Spoon in ⅕ of the chicken mixture on the bottom. Top with ⅕ of the cheese and then 1 tortilla. Continue layering in that order, and with those amounts, 4 more times, ending with cheese on top.

4. Cover cooker and cook on Low 4 hours.

Greek Chicken Pita Filling

Judi Manos
West Islip, NY

Jeanette Oberholtzer
Manheim, PA

Makes 4 servings
Prep. Time: 10 minutes ⚶ *Cooking Time: 6–8 hours* ⚶ *Ideal slow-cooker size: 2- to 3-qt.*

I onion, chopped
I lb. boneless, skinless chicken thighs
I tsp. lemon pepper
½ tsp. dried oregano
½ cup plain yogurt

1. Combine first 3 ingredients in slow cooker. Cover and cook on Low 6–8 hours, or until chicken is tender.

2. Just before serving, remove chicken and shred with two forks.

3. Add shredded chicken back into slow cooker and stir in oregano and yogurt.

Serving suggestion:
Serve as a filling for pita bread.

Easy Creamy Chicken

Karen Waggoner
Joplin, MO

Makes 8 servings
Prep. Time: 5 minutes ❧ *Cooking Time: 2–4 hours* ❧ *Ideal slow-cooker size: 4-qt.*

8 boneless, skinless chicken breast halves

lemon pepper to taste

10¾-oz. can cream of chicken soup

3-oz. pkg. cream cheese, softened

8-oz. carton sour cream

1. Place 4 breasts in bottom of slow cooker. Sprinkle with lemon pepper.

2. Mix soup and cream cheese together in a bowl. When blended, fold in sour cream.

3. Pour half the sauce over the breasts in the cooker.

4. Repeat steps 1 and 3.

5. Cover and cook on High for 2–4 hours, or until chicken is tender but not dry.

Serving suggestion:

This is good served over cooked rice.

Simply Delicious Chicken Breasts

Donna Treloar
Hartford City, IN

Makes 4 servings
Prep. Time: 3 minutes ⚘ *Cooking Time: 4–6 hours* ⚘ *Ideal slow-cooker size: 3-qt.*

4 bone-in chicken breast halves, or chicken legs and thighs

10¾-oz. can golden mushroom soup

1 envelope dry onion soup mix

1. Place chicken in slow cooker.

2. Pour soup over chicken. Sprinkle with dry soup mix.

3. Cover and cook on Low 4–6 hours, or until chicken is tender but not dry.

Lemon Pepper Chicken and Veggies

Nadine Martinitz
Salina, KS

Makes 4 servings
Prep. Time: 20 minutes ❧ *Cooking Time: 4–10 hours* ❧ *Ideal slow-cooker size: 4-qt.*

4 carrots, sliced ½-inch thick

4 potatoes, cut in 1-inch chunks

2 cloves garlic, peeled and minced, *optional*

4 whole chicken legs and thighs, skin removed

2 tsp. lemon pepper seasoning

¼–½ tsp. poultry seasoning, *optional*

14½-oz. can chicken broth

1. Layer vegetables and chicken in slow cooker.

2. Sprinkle with lemon pepper seasoning, and poultry seasoning if you wish. Pour broth over all.

3. Cover and cook on Low 8–10 hours or on High 4–5 hours.

Variations:

1. Use a 10¾-oz. can cream of chicken or mushroom soup instead of chicken broth.

   —Sarah Herr, Goshen, IN

2. Add 2 cups frozen green beans to the bottom layer (Step 1) in the cooker.

   —Earnest Zimmerman, Mechanicsburg, PA

Sunday Chicken Dinner

Beverly Flatt-Getz
Warriors Mark, PA

Makes 4 servings
Prep. Time: 15–20 minutes ⚓ Cooking Time: 4–8 hours ⚓ Ideal slow-cooker size: 4- to 5-qt.

1 large onion, sliced

4–5 potatoes, peeled and sliced about ¼-inch thick

3–4 lbs. chicken, cut up

10¾-oz. can cream of mushroom soup

1 soup can of milk

garlic powder to taste, *optional*

1. Line bottom of your slow cooker with onion slices.

2. Spread potatoes over top of onions. Then add chicken.

3. Mix together soup and milk. Pour over chicken.

4. If you wish, sprinkle with garlic powder.

5. Cook on High 4 hours or on Low 8 hours, or until potatoes and chicken are tender.

Tip:

Add up to a second can of milk if you'd like to have more sauce.

Slow-Cooker Chicken and Gravy

Betty Moore
Plano, IL

Makes 6–8 servings
Prep. Time: 5 minutes & Cooking Time: 6 hours & Ideal slow-cooker size: 4-qt.

6–8 bone-in chicken breast halves
salt and pepper to taste
10¾-oz. can cream of mushroom soup
1 Tbsp. flour
½ cup water
paprika to taste

1. Season chicken breasts with salt and pepper. Place in slow cooker.

2. Pour soup over chicken.

3. Cover and cook on Low 6 hours.

4. Remove chicken to a serving dish or platter. Cover to keep warm.

5. Turn slow cooker to High. In a small mixing bowl, blend flour into water until smooth. Stir into hot gravy in slow cooker.

6. Cook until thickened. Pour over chicken to serve.

7. Sprinkle with paprika just before serving.

Chicken with Vegetables

Janie Steele
Moore, OK

Makes 4 servings
Prep. Time: 10–15 minutes   ❧   *Cooking Time: 6–8 hours*   ❧   *Ideal slow-cooker size: 6-qt.*

4 bone-in chicken breast halves

1 small head of cabbage, quartered

1-lb. pkg. baby carrots

2 (14½-oz.) cans Mexican-style stewed tomatoes

1. Place all ingredients in slow cooker in order listed.

2. Cover and cook on Low 6–8 hours, or until chicken and vegetables are tender.

Chicken and Stuffing

Karen Waggoner
Joplin, MO

Makes 4 servings
Prep. Time: 5 minutes   ❧   *Cooking Time: 2–2½ hours*   ❧   *Ideal slow-cooker size: 4-qt.*

4 boneless, skinless chicken breast halves

6-oz. box stuffing mix for chicken

16-oz. pkg. frozen whole-kernel corn

4 Tbsp. (½ stick) butter, melted

2 cups water

1. Place chicken in bottom of slow cooker.

2. Mix remaining ingredients together in a mixing bowl. Spoon over chicken.

3. Cover and cook on High 2–2½ hours, or until chicken is tender and the stuffing is dry.

Creamy Baked Chicken with Stuffing

Vera Martin
East Earl, PA

Makes 8 servings
Prep. Time: 10–15 minutes ⚬ *Cooking Time: 4½ hours* ⚬ *Ideal slow-cooker size: 6-qt.*

8 boneless chicken breast halves, divided

10¾-oz. can cream of chicken soup

¼ cup water

1 cup crushed herb-seasoned stuffing

4 Tbsp. (½ stick) butter, melted

7 slices white American cheese

1. Lightly grease slow cooker. Layer half the chicken in bottom of slow cooker.

2. In a small bowl, mix soup and water together. Spoon half of the sauce over the chicken in the cooker.

3. Layer remaining 4 breasts into cooker. Top with remaining sauce.

4. Sprinkle stuffing crumbs over top. Drizzle with melted butter.

5. Cover and cook on High for 4 hours, or until chicken is tender.

6. Place cheese slices over crumbs. Cover and cook another 30 minutes.

Chicken and Rice Casserole

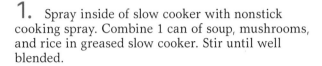

Dale Peterson
Rapid City, SD

Joyce M. Shackelford
Green Bay, WI

Makes 3–4 servings
Prep. Time: 20 minutes ❧ Cooking Time: 4–5 hours ❧ Ideal slow-cooker size: 6-qt.

2 (10¾-oz.) cans cream of celery soup, *divided*

2-oz. can sliced mushrooms, undrained

½ cup raw long-grain rice

2 whole boneless, skinless chicken breasts, uncooked and cubed

1 Tbsp. dry onion soup mix

½ soup can water

1. Spray inside of slow cooker with nonstick cooking spray. Combine 1 can of soup, mushrooms, and rice in greased slow cooker. Stir until well blended.

2. Lay chicken on top. Pour 1 can of soup over all.

3. Sprinkle with onion soup mix. Add ½ soup can of water.

4. Cover and cook on Low 4–5 hours, or until both chicken and rice are fully cooked but not dry.

Chicken with Broccoli Rice

Maryann Markano
Wilmington, DE

Makes 6 servings
Prep. Time: 20 minutes ᛤ *Cooking Time: 6–8 hours* ᛤ *Ideal slow-cooker size: 5-qt.*

1¼ cups uncooked long-grain rice

pepper to taste

2 lbs. boneless, skinless chicken breasts, cut into strips

1 pkg. Knorr cream of broccoli dry soup mix

2½ cups chicken broth

1. Spray slow cooker with nonstick cooking spray. Place rice in cooker. Sprinkle with pepper.

2. Top with chicken pieces.

3. In a mixing bowl, combine soup mix and broth. Pour over chicken and rice.

4. Cover and cook on Low 6–8 hours, or until rice and chicken are tender but not dry.

Beef

All-Day Pot Roast

Carol Shirk
Leola, PA

Makes 5 servings
Prep. Time: 15–20 minutes ⚶ *Cooking Time: 5–12 hours* ⚶ *Ideal slow-cooker size: 4-qt.*

4 medium-sized potatoes, quartered

16-oz. pkg. peeled baby carrots

1½-lb. boneless eye of beef round roast, round rump roast, or chuck roast, browned if you have access to a stove

10¾-oz. can golden mushroom soup

½ tsp. dried tarragon, or basil, crushed

1. Place potatoes and carrots in slow cooker. Place beef on top of vegetables.

2. In a small bowl, mix together soup and tarragon or basil. Pour over meat and vegetables.

3. Cover and cook on Low 10–12 hours, or on High 5–6 hours, until meat and vegetables are tender but not dry.

Whole Dinner Roast Beef

Betty Moore
Plano, IL

Rhonda Freed
Lowville, NY

Makes 6–8 servings
Prep. Time: 10 minutes ⚘ *Cooking Time: 8–9 hours* ⚘ *Ideal slow-cooker size: 3½- to 4-qt.*

3–5-lb. beef roast
10¾-oz. can cream of mushroom soup
1 envelope dry onion soup mix
4 cups baby carrots
4–5 potatoes, quartered

1. Place the roast in your slow cooker.

2. Cover with mushroom soup. Sprinkle with onion soup mix.

3. Cover and cook on Low 6 hours.

4. Add carrots and potatoes, pushing down into the sauce as much as possible.

5. Cover and cook another 2–3 hours, or until vegetables are tender, but meat is not dry.

Variations:

1. Sprinkle carrots and potatoes with salt and pepper after placing in cooker.

2. Stir a soup can of water into the mushroom soup before adding to cooker in Step 2.

Cozy Cabin Casserole

Anna Musser
Manheim, PA

Makes 3–4 servings
Prep. Time: 5 minutes ⚯ Cooking Time: 6–8 hours ⚯ Ideal slow-cooker size: 4-qt.

1 lb. lean round steak
1 envelope dry onion soup mix
10¾-oz. can cream of mushroom soup
10¾-oz. can cream of celery soup
½ cup sour cream

1. Layer first four ingredients in slow cooker.

2. Cover and cook on Low 6–8 hours, or until meat is tender but not overcooked.

3. Stir in sour cream 10 minutes before serving.

Swiss Steak and Gravy

Sherry H. Kauffman
Minot, ND

Ruth Retter
Manheim, PA

Chris Peterson
Green Bay, WI

Mary Lynn Miller
Reinholds, PA

Virginia Eberly
Loysville, PA

Wilma J. Haberkamp
Fairbank, IA

Phyllis Wykes
Plano, IL

Esther Burkholder
Millerstown, PA

Paula King
Flanagan, IL

Lois Ostrander
Lebanon, PA

Makes 6–8 servings
Prep. Time: 5 minutes ⚜ *Cooking Time: 4–7 hours* ⚜ *Ideal slow-cooker size: 5-qt.*

2–2½-lb. round steak, cut into serving-size pieces

10¾-oz. can cream of mushroom soup

½ soup can milk or water

½–1 envelope dry onion soup mix, depending upon your taste preference

1. Place steak in slow cooker.

2. In a bowl, mix soup and milk together. Pour over steak.

3. Sprinkle dry onion soup mix over top.

4. Cover and cook on Low 4–7 hours, or until the meat is tender but not overcooked.

Variations:

1. Add a 4-oz. can sliced mushrooms, drained, on top of the steak, in Step 1. Sprinkle the top of the dish with ¼ tsp. black pepper at the end of Step 3.

—Bonnie Goering, Bridgewater, VA

2. Cut the steak into 2x4-inch strips. Toss with mushroom soup mixture. Place in slow cooker and proceed with Step 4.

—Sheila Soldner, Lititz, PA

3. Use cubed steak instead of round steak. And use 1 cup water instead of only half a soup can.

—Sara Kinsinger, Stuarts Draft, VA

Slow-Cooked Swiss Steak

Kathy Lapp
Halifax, PA

Makes 4–6 servings
Prep. Time: 15 minutes & *Cooking Time: 4–5 hours* & *Ideal slow-cooker size: 4-qt.*

1¾-lb. round steak
¼ cup flour
2 onions, sliced thick
1 green pepper, sliced in strips
10¾-oz. can cream of mushroom soup

1. Cut steak into serving-size pieces. Dredge in flour. If a stove top is available, brown steak in a nonstick skillet.

2. Place steak in slow cooker. Top with onion and pepper slices.

3. Pour soup over all, making sure steak pieces are covered.

4. Cover and cook on Low 4–5 hours.

Variations:

1. Add ½ tsp. salt and ¼ tsp. pepper to flour in Step 1.

2. If you like a lot of gravy, add a second can of soup to Step 3.

Zesty French Dip

Earnest Zimmerman
Mechanicsburg, PA

Tracey Hanson Schramel
Windom, MN

Makes 6–8 servings
Prep. Time: 5 minutes   Cooking Time: 8 hours   Ideal slow-cooker size: 4- to 6-qt.

4-lb. beef roast

10½-oz. can beef broth

10½-oz. can condensed French onion soup

12-oz. bottle of beer

6–8 French rolls or baguettes

1. Pat roast dry and place in slow cooker.

2. In a mixing bowl, combine beef broth, onion soup, and beer. Pour over meat.

3. Cover and cook on Low 8 hours, or until meat is tender but not dry.

4. Split rolls or baguettes. Warm in the oven, microwave, or over the campfire until heated through.

5. Remove meat from cooker and allow to rest for 10 minutes. Then shred with two forks, or cut on the diagonal into thin slices and place in rolls. Serve with dipping sauce on the side.

Italian Beef

Peggy Forsythe
Bartlett, TN

Makes 6 servings
Prep. Time: 20 minutes ♣ *Cooking Time: 8 hours* ♣ *Ideal slow-cooker size: 4- to 6-qt.*

4–5-lb. beef roast, cut into 1–1½-inch cubes

2–3 beef bouillon cubes

1 tsp. garlic salt

2 Tbsp. Italian salad dressing

1. Place roast, bouillon cubes, garlic salt, and dressing in slow cooker. Stir.

2. Add 1–1½ inches water around the beef, being careful not to disturb the seasoning on the top of the meat.

3. Cover and cook on Low 8 hours, or until tender but not overcooked.

4. Remove beef from cooker and shred with 2 forks. Return shredded meat to cooker and stir into broth.

5. Serve over rice, or on rolls or garlic bread for a delicious open-face sandwich.

Roast Beef Sandwiches

Kelly Bailey
Mechanicsburg, PA

Makes 10–12 servings
Prep. Time: 15 minutes 🦴 Cooking Time: 24 hours 🦴 Ideal slow-cooker size: 3-qt.

3 lb. beef roast

14¾-oz. can beef broth

1 envelope dry Italian salad dressing mix

10–12 crusty sandwich rolls

Optional ingredients:

½ cup mayonnaise

3 Tbsp. prepared mustard

1. Place beef in slow cooker.

2. Combine broth and dressing mix and pour mixture over beef.

3. Cover and cook on Low 12 hours.

4. Remove beef from broth and shred with 2 forks.

5. Return shredded beef to slow cooker and continue to cook on Low for another 12 hours.

6. Serve in crusty rolls, along with mayonnaise mixed with mustard, if you wish.

Spicy French Dip

Joette Droz
Kalona, IA

Makes 10–12 servings
Prep. Time: 10 minutes ⚬ *Cooking Time: 8–10 hours* ⚬ *Ideal slow-cooker size: 4-qt.*

3-lb. boneless beef roast, cut in thirds

½ cup water

4-oz. can diced jalapeño peppers, drained

1 envelope dry Italian salad dressing mix

10–12 crusty sandwich rolls

1. Place 3 pieces of beef in slow cooker.

2. In a small bowl, combine the water, jalapeños, and dry dressing mix. Pour over beef.

3. Cover and cook on Low 8–10 hours, or until meat is tender but not dry.

4. Remove beef and shred using 2 forks. Place shredded beef back in juices. Stir and serve on rolls.

Beef Brisket Barbecue

Sharon Timpe
Jackson, WI

Makes 8 servings
Prep. Time: 15 minutes ⚜ Cooking Time: 6¼–7¼ hours ⚜ Ideal slow-cooker size: 4- to 5-qt.

2 cups barbecue sauce, *divided*
1 small onion, chopped
3 tsp. beef bouillon granules, or 2 beef bouillon cubes
3–4-lb. boneless beef brisket
8 sandwich rolls

Tip:

You can also serve the beef brisket barbecue on small buns as a snack or appetizer. Serving from the slow cooker keeps the meat hot, and guests can help themselves whenever they want to.

1. In the bottom of your slow cooker combine 1 cup barbecue sauce, chopped onion, and bouillon.

2. Place beef brisket on top.

3. Cover and cook on Low 6–7 hours, or until brisket shreds easily.

4. Remove brisket from cooker. Using 2 forks, shred the meat.

5. Tilt cooker and spoon off fat from cooking broth. Discard fat.

6. Pour cooking broth into a bowl. Again, spoon off any remaining fat and discard.

7. Measure out 1 cup of cooking broth. Pour back into slow cooker, along with remaining cup of barbecue sauce. Blend broth and sauce well.

8. Return shredded meat to slow cooker. Stir into sauce thoroughly.

9. Cover and cook on High for 15 minutes, or until meat is hot.

10. Serve over sandwich rolls.

Barbecued Beef Sandwiches

Arianne Hochstetler
Goshen, IN

Makes 24 servings
Prep. Time: 15 minutes ⚮ Cooking Time: 5½–6½ hours ⚮ Ideal slow-cooker size: 4-qt.

4-lb. round steak, ¾-inch thick, cut into 3-inch cubes
2 cups ketchup
1 cup cola
½ cup chopped onion
2 cloves garlic, minced

1. Spray slow cooker with nonstick cooking spray.

2. Place beef pieces in cooker.

3. Mix remaining ingredients in a large bowl and pour over meat.

4. Cover and cook on High 5–6 hours.

5. About 30 minutes before serving, remove beef from slow cooker and shred with 2 forks. Return beef to slow cooker and mix well with sauce.

6. Cover and cook on High an additional 20 minutes.

Serving suggestion:
Spoon about ⅓ cup beef mixture into individual sandwich buns.

Pulled Beef or Pork

Pat Bechtel
Dillsburg, PA

Makes 16–18 servings
Prep. Time: 5–10 minutes ⚬ *Cooking Time: 8–10 hours* ⚬ *Ideal slow-cooker size: 3½-qt.*

4-lb. beef or pork roast
2 envelopes dry ranch dressing mix
2 envelopes dry Italian dressing mix

1. Cook roast in slow cooker on Low for 8–10 hours, or until tender but not overcooked. Do not add water or seasonings! By the end of the cooking time there will be broth from cooking—do not discard it!

2. Just before serving remove meat from slow cooker. Using 2 forks, pull meat apart.

3. Add dry dressing mixes to broth and stir thoroughly. Stir pulled meat back into broth in the cooker. Serve immediately in rolls, or over cooked rice or pasta, or over mashed potatoes.

Super Beef Barbecue

Linda E. Wilcox
Blythewood, SC

Makes 10–12 servings
Prep. Time: 15 minutes ⚬ Cooking Time: 9–10 hours ⚬ Ideal slow-cooker size: 6-qt.

3–4-lb. rump roast

1 clove garlic, minced, or ¼ cup finely chopped onion

18-oz. bottle barbecue sauce

1 cup ketchup

16-oz. jar whole dill pickles, undrained

1. Cut roast into quarters and place in slow cooker.

2. In a bowl, stir together garlic, barbecue sauce, and ketchup. When well blended, fold in pickles and their juice. Pour over meat.

3. Cover and cook on Low 8–9 hours, or until meat begins to fall apart.

4. Remove the pickles and discard them.

5. Lift the meat out onto a platter and shred by pulling it apart with 2 forks.

6. Return meat to sauce and heat thoroughly on Low, about 1 hour.

Serving suggestion:
Serve in sandwich rolls.

Easy Meatloaf

Karen Waggoner
Joplin, MO

Makes 5–6 servings
Prep. Time: 5 minutes ⚬ Cooking Time: 2 hours ⚬ Ideal slow-cooker size: 3- to 4-qt.

2 lbs. ground beef or turkey

6¼-oz. pkg. stuffing mix for beef, plus seasoning

2 eggs, beaten

½ cup ketchup, *divided*

1. Mix beef or turkey, dry stuffing, eggs, and ¼ cup ketchup. Shape into an oval loaf.

2. Place in slow cooker. Pour remaining ketchup over top.

3. Cover and cook on High for 2 hours.

Meatloaf

Becky Gehman
Bergton, VA

Makes 6–8 servings
Prep. Time: 10 minutes ⚜ *Cooking Time: 2–6 hours* ⚜ *Ideal slow-cooker size: 3-qt.*

2 lbs. ground beef
½ cup cracker crumbs
1–2 tsp. onion powder
¼ cup ketchup

1. Combine ground beef, cracker crumbs, and onion powder. Form into a loaf. Place in your slow cooker.

2. Spread ketchup over top of meatloaf.

3. Cover and cook on Low for 4–6 hours, or on High for 2 hours.

Tips:

1. You may mix all or half the ketchup into the meatloaf.

2. Remove the cooked meatloaf from the cooker with a slotted spoon, and keep it warm on a platter. Pour the drippings from the slow cooker into a nonstick skillet, if you have access to a stove top. Turn the burner to medium and whisk 2 Tbsp. flour into the drippings until smooth. Add a beef bouillon cube and stir until the cube is dissolved and the drippings thicken. Serve the gravy with the sliced meatloaf.

Easy Hamburgers

Hope Comerford
Clinton Township, MI

Makes 8–9 3-inch patties
Prep. Time: 20 minutes ⚬ Cooking Time: 4–5 hours ⚬ Ideal slow-cooker size: 6 to 7-qt.

¼ cup water

2 lbs. ground beef

I cup Italian seasoned bread crumbs

I-oz. pkg. Hidden Valley Ranch Salad Dressing & Seasoning Mix

I-oz. pkg. Lipton Onion Soup Mix

I egg

I Tbsp. Worcestershire sauce

1. Crumple up some foil in the bottom of the crock. This will keep the burgers from cooking in the grease. Pour the water into the bottom of the crock.

2. In a bowl, mix together the ground beef, bread crumbs, ranch dressing mix, onion soup mix, egg, and Worcestershire sauce. Form the burgers into 3-inch patties.

3. Place enough patties onto the crumpled foil that just covers the bottom. Do not overlap the patties.

4. Fold some foil into strips and make a star shape, crisscrossing them over one another, on top of the patties already in the crock. Lay the remaining patties on top.

5. Cover and cook on Low for 4–5 hours.

Creamy Sloppy Joes

Clara Yoder Byler
Hartville, OH

Makes 8–10 servings
Prep. Time: 30 minutes ⚜ *Cooking Time: 2–3 hours* ⚜ *Ideal slow-cooker size: 4-qt.*

2 lbs. ground beef
1 onion, finely chopped
½ cup ketchup
1 tsp. Worcestershire sauce
10¾-oz. can cream of mushroom soup
1 tsp. salt, *optional*
rolls

1. If you have access to a stove top, brown the beef in a nonstick skillet and then drain.

2. Combine all ingredients except rolls in the slow cooker.

3. Cover and cook on High for 2–3 hours, or until heated through.

4. Serve in rolls.

Sloppy Joes

Rosalie D. Miller
Mifflintown, PA

Makes 8–10 servings
Prep. Time: 10–15 minutes ⚘ Cooking Time: 3–8 hours ⚘ Ideal slow-cooker size: 3- to 4-qt.

3 lbs. ground beef
1 cup chopped onions
3 (16-oz.) cans sloppy joe sauce
4 Tbsp. brown sugar
4 Tbsp. Worcestershire sauce
hamburger buns

1. If you have access to a stove top, brown the beef in a nonstick skillet and then drain.

2. Combine all ingredients, except hamburger buns, in the slow cooker.

3. Cover and cook on Low for 6–8 hours, or on High for 3–4 hours.

4. Spoon mixture into hamburger buns to serve.

Easy Crock Taco Filling

Joanne Good
Wheaton, IL

Makes 4–6 servings
Prep. Time: 20 minutes   ❧   Cooking Time: 6–8 hours   ❧   Ideal slow-cooker size: 4-qt.

1 lb. ground beef
1 large onion, chopped
2 (15-oz.) cans chili beans
15-oz. can Santa Fe style corn, or Mexican, or Fiesta corn
¾ cup water
Optional ingredients:
¼ tsp. cayenne pepper
½ tsp. garlic powder

1. If you have access to a stove top, brown the beef in a nonstick skillet and then drain.

2. Mix all ingredients together in the slow cooker, blending well.

3. Cover and cook on Low for 6–8 hours.

Tip:

You may want to add more or less than ¾ cup water to this recipe, depending upon how hot and fast your slow cooker cooks and how tight-fitting its lid is.

Serving suggestions:

1. Serve in warmed, soft corn tortillas or hard taco shells. Or, serve as a taco dip with plain corn tortilla chips.

2. Good garnishes for this taco filling include sour cream, guacamole, shredded cheese, diced tomatoes, shredded lettuce, and salsa.

Easy Beef Tortillas

Karen Waggoner
Joplin, MO

Makes 6 servings
Prep. Time: 20 minutes ♣ Cooking Time:1½–3 hours ♣ Ideal slow-cooker size: 4-qt.

1½ lbs. ground beef

10¾-oz. can cream of chicken soup

2½ cups crushed tortilla chips, *divided*

16-oz. jar salsa

1½ cups (6 oz.) shredded cheddar cheese

1. If you have access to a stove top, brown the beef in a nonstick skillet and then drain.

2. In a bowl, combine the beef and soup. Set aside.

3. Spray inside of cooker with nonstick cooking spray. Sprinkle 1½ cups tortilla chips in slow cooker. Top with beef mixture, then salsa, and then cheese.

4. Cover and cook on High for 1½ hours, or on Low for 3 hours.

5. Sprinkle with remaining chips just before serving.

Pork

Pork Butt Roast

Instant Pot

Marla Folkerts
Batavia, IL

Makes 6–8 servings
Prep. Time: 10 minutes ⚬ Cooking Time: 9 minutes ⚬
Setting: Manual ⚬ Pressure: High ⚬ Release: Natural

3–4-lb. pork butt roast

2–3 Tbsp. of your favorite rub

2 cups water

1. Place pork in the inner pot of the Instant Pot.

2. Sprinkle in the rub all over the roast and add the water, being careful not to wash off the rub.

3. Secure the lid and set the vent to sealing. Cook for 9 minutes on the Manual setting.

4. Let the pressure release naturally.

Pork Roast

Kelly Bailey
Mechanicsburg, PA

Makes 8–10 servings
Prep. Time: 5 minutes ⚬ Cooking Time: 6–12 hours ⚬ Ideal slow-cooker size: 4- to 6-qt.

medium to large onion, sliced and divided

3–4-lb. pork roast

12-oz. can cola

salt and pepper

1. Layer ⅔ of the onion slices in bottom of slow cooker, reserving a few to place on top of roast.

2. Place roast in cooker. Pour cola over roast.

3. Season with salt and pepper and top with remaining onion slices.

4. Cook on Low 6–12 hours depending on size of roast, until meat starts to fall apart.

Hassle-Free Pork Chops

Cathy Sellers
Cedar Rapids, IA

Makes 4 servings

Prep. Time: 15 minutes & Cooking Time: 3–8 hours & Ideal slow-cooker size: 3- to 4-qt.

4 pork chops

1 small onion, sliced

4 potatoes, peeled and sliced

2 (10¾-oz.) cans tomato soup

½ cup milk

1. Heat a nonstick skillet on the stove-top until hot. Add chops and brown on both sides. Do in batches rather than crowd the skillet. If you do not have access to a stove top, you may skip to Step 2.

2. Place chops in slow cooker. If a stove top is available, brown onion in skillet drippings, and then place over top of chops. If not, simply add onions to the cooker.

3. Add layer of potatoes to the cooker.

4. In a small bowl, combine soup and milk, mixing well. Pour mixture over potatoes.

5. Cover and cook on Low 6–8 hours, or on High 3–4 hours, or until meat and potatoes are tender but not dry.

Variation:

Add salt and pepper to taste to the chops as you place them in the slow cooker. Add more salt and pepper to taste to the layer of sliced potatoes after you've placed them in the cooker.

Carolina Pot Roast

Jonathan Gehman
Harrisonburg, VA

Makes 3–4 servings
Prep. Time: 20 minutes ♣ Cooking Time: 3 hours ♣ Ideal slow-cooker size: 3-qt.

3 medium-large sweet potatoes, peeled and cut into 1-inch chunks

½ cup brown sugar

1-lb. pork roast

scant ¼ tsp. cumin

salt to taste

water

1. Place sweet potatoes in bottom of slow cooker. Sprinkle brown sugar over potatoes.

2. If you have access to a stove top, heat a nonstick skillet over medium-high heat. Add roast and brown on all sides. Sprinkle meat with cumin and salt while browning. Place pork on top of potatoes. If you do not have access to a stove top to brown the meat, simply season the roast with the cumin and salt and place on top of the potatoes.

3. Add an inch of water to the cooker, being careful not to wash the seasoning off the meat.

4. Cover and cook on Low 3 hours, or until meat and potatoes are tender but not dry or mushy.

Creamy Pork Chops

Judi Manos
West Islip, NY

Makes 6 servings
Prep. Time: 5–7 minutes ⚬ *Cooking Time: 4–5 hours* ⚬ *Ideal slow-cooker size: 3-qt.*

10¾-oz. can 98% fat-free cream of chicken soup

1 onion, chopped

3 Tbsp. ketchup

2 tsp. Worcestershire sauce

6 whole pork chops, boneless or bone-in, *divided*

1. Mix soup and chopped onion together in a bowl. Stir in ketchup and Worcestershire sauce. Pour ½ of mixture into slow cooker.

2. Place pork chops in slow cooker. If you have to stack them, spoon a proportionate amount of the remaining sauce over the first layer of meat.

3. Add the rest of the chops. Cover with the remaining sauce.

4. Cover and cook on Low 4–5 hours, or until meat is tender but not dry.

Honey Barbecue Pork Chops

Tamara McCarthy
Pennsburg, PA

Makes 8 servings
Prep. Time: 15 minutes ⚬ Cooking Time: 6–8 hours ⚬ Ideal slow-cooker size: 4-qt.

8 pork chops, *divided*

1 large onion, sliced, *divided*

1 cup barbecue sauce

⅓ cup honey

1. Place one layer of pork chops in your slow cooker.

2. Arrange a proportionate amount of sliced onion over top.

3. Mix barbecue sauce and honey together in a small bowl. Spoon a proportionate amount of sauce over the chops.

4. Repeat the layers.

5. Cover and cook on Low 3–4 hours.

6. If the sauce barely covers the chops, flip them over at this point. If they're well covered, simply allow them to cook another 3–4 hours on Low, or until they're tender but the meat is not dry.

Tender Tasty Ribs

Instant Pot

Carol Eveleth
Cheyenne, WY

Makes 2–3 servings
Prep. Time: 5 minutes ⚘ Cooking Time: 35 minutes ⚘
Setting: Manual ⚘ Pressure: High ⚘ Release: Natural

2 tsp. salt

2 tsp. black pepper

I tsp. garlic powder

I tsp. onion powder

I slab baby back ribs

I cup water

I cup barbecue sauce, *divided*

1. Mix salt, pepper, garlic powder, and onion powder together. Rub seasoning mixture on both sides of slab of ribs. Cut slab in half if it's too big for your Instant Pot.

2. Pour water into inner pot of the Instant Pot. Place ribs into pot, drizzle with ¼ cup of sauce, and secure lid. Make sure the vent is set to sealing.

3. Set it to Manual for 25 minutes. It will take a few minutes to heat up and seal the vent. When cook time is up, let it sit 5 minutes, then release steam by turning valve to venting. Turn oven on to broil (or heat your grill) while you're waiting for the 5-minute resting time.

4. Remove ribs from Instant Pot and place on a baking sheet. Slather on both sides with remaining ¾ cup sauce.

5. Place under broiler (or on grill) for 5–10 minutes, watching carefully so it doesn't burn. Remove and brush with a bit more sauce. Pull apart and dig in!

Barbecued Ribs

Sara Harter Fredette
Goshen, MA

Margaret H. Moffitt
Bartlett, TN

Makes 6 servings
Prep. Time: 2 minutes   ❧   Cooking Time: 5–6 hours   ❧   Ideal slow-cooker size: 4- to 5-qt.

6 lean pork ribs, or chops

salt and pepper to taste

19-oz. bottle hickory, or sweet and tangy, barbecue sauce

1. Place meat in slow cooker; cut the ribs to fit. Sprinkle each piece with salt and pepper.

2. If you need to create layers of meat, be sure to top each section of ribs with a proportionate amount of sauce.

3. Cover and cook on High for 1 hour. Then cook on Low for 4–5 hours, or until meat is tender, but not dry.

4. When ready to serve, remove ribs from cooker and place on serving platter. Cover to keep warm. Tilt cooker in order to be able to spoon off any fat that has floated to the top of the sauce. Then spoon sauce over ribs and serve any extra in a separate bowl.

Variations:

1. If you have access to an oven, broil the ribs for about 5–15 minutes per side, about 6 inches below the broiler heat, before placing them in the cooker. The browning adds depth of flavor and also cooks off some of the fat.

—Corinna Herr, Stevens, PA

—Margaret Culbert, Lebanon, PA

—Dorothy Lingerfelt, Stonyford, CA

2. Slice one medium-sized onion. Then lay the slices into the bottom of the cooker before adding the meat.

—Corinna Herr, Stevens, PA

—Karen Ceneviva, New Haven, CT

—Audrey Romonosky, Austin, TX

Shredded Pork

Cindy Krestynick
Glen Lyon, PA

Makes 6–8 servings
Prep. Time: 10 minutes ⚘ *Cooking Time: 4–10 hours* ⚘ *Ideal slow-cooker size: 4- to 5-qt.*

3–4-lb. pork butt roast

1½ envelopes taco seasoning

3–5 cloves garlic, according to your taste preference, sliced

1 large onion, quartered

4-oz. can whole green chiles, drained

1 cup water

1. Place roast in slow cooker.

2. In a bowl, mix all remaining ingredients together. Spoon over meat in cooker.

3. Cover and cook on Low for 8–10 hours, or on High 4–6 hours, or until meat is tender but not dry.

4. Place pork on a platter and shred with 2 forks. Stir shredded meat back into sauce.

Serving suggestion:
Serve in tortillas, topped with shredded lettuce, tomato, and sour cream, or over steamed rice.

Pulled Pork

Instant Pot

Colleen Heatwole
Burton, MI

Makes 8 servings
Prep. Time: 15 minutes & Cooking Time: 75 minutes &
Setting: Meat/Stew & Pressure: High & Release: Natural

2 Tbsp. vegetable oil

4-lb. boneless pork shoulder, cut into two pieces

2 cups barbecue sauce, *divided*

½ cup water

1. Add oil to the inner pot of the Instant Pot and select Sauté.

2. When oil is hot, brown pork on both sides, about 3 minutes per side. Brown each half of roast separately. Remove to platter when browned.

3. Add 1 cup barbecue sauce and ½ cup water to the inner pot. Stir to combine.

4. Add browned pork and any accumulated juices to the inner pot. Secure the lid and set vent to sealing.

5. Using Meat/Stew mode, set timer to 60 minutes, on high pressure.

6. When cook time is up, allow the pressure to release naturally.

7. Carefully remove meat and shred with two forks, discarding excess fat as you shred.

8. Strain cooking liquid, reserving ½ cup. If possible, use a fat separator to separate fat from juices.

9. Place shredded pork in the inner pot with remaining 1 cup barbecue sauce and reserved ½ cup cooking liquid. Using Sauté function, stir to combine and bring to a simmer, stirring frequently.

BBQ Pork Sandwiches

Instant Pot

Carol Eveleth
Cheyenne, WY

Makes 4 servings
Prep. Time: 20 minutes ⚬ *Cooking Time: 1 hour* ⚬
Setting: Manual and Sauté ⚬ *Pressure: High* ⚬ *Release: Manual*

2 tsp. salt

I tsp. onion powder

I tsp. garlic powder

2-lb. pork shoulder roast, cut into 3-inch pieces

I Tbsp. olive oil

2 cups barbecue sauce

1. In a small bowl, combine the salt, onion powder, and garlic powder. Season the pork with the rub.

2. Turn the Instant Pot on to Sauté. Heat the olive oil in the inner pot.

3. Add the pork to the oil and turn to coat. Lock the lid and set vent to sealing.

4. Press Manual and cook on high pressure for 45 minutes.

5. When cooking is complete, release the pressure manually, then open the lid.

6. Using 2 forks, shred the pork, pour barbecue sauce over the pork, then press Sauté. Simmer, 3–5 minutes. Press Cancel. Toss pork to mix.

Serving suggestion:

Pile the shredded BBQ pork on the bottom half of a bun. Add any additional toppings if you wish, then finish with the top half of the bun.

Hot Dogs

Hope Comerford
Clinton Township, MI

Makes 8 or more

Prep. Time: 2 minutes ⚬ Cooking Time: 1–4 hours ⚬ Ideal slow-cooker size: 3-qt.

8 or more hot dogs (as many as you wish and will fit in your crock)

8 or more hot dog buns

1. Place hot dogs in the crock vertically (standing on end) if you're making a bunch or horizontally (lying flat) if you're only making 8.

2. Cover and cook on High 1–2 hours or Low 3–4 hours.

3. Serve in hot dog buns with your favorite toppings.

Side Dishes & Vegetables

Corn on the Cob

Donna Conto
Saylorsburg, PA

Makes 3–4 servings
Prep. Time: 10 minutes   ⚬   Cooking Time: 2–3 hours   ⚬   Ideal slow-cooker size: 5- or 6-qt.

6–8 ears of corn (in husk)

½ cup water

1. Remove silk from corn, as much as possible, but leave husks on.

2. Cut off ends of corn so ears can stand in the cooker.

3. Add water.

4. Cover. Cook on Low 2–3 hours.

Chili Lime Corn on the Cob

Hope Comerford
Clinton Township, MI

Makes 6 servings
Prep. Time: 10 minutes ⚓ *Cooking Time: 4 hours* ⚓ *Ideal slow-cooker size: 6-qt.*

6 ears of corn, shucked and cleaned

6 Tbsp. butter, room temperature

2 Tbsp. freshly squeezed lime juice

1 tsp. lime zest

2 tsp. chili powder

1 tsp. salt

½ tsp. pepper

1. Tear off six pieces of aluminum foil to fit each ear of corn. Place each ear of corn on a piece of foil.

2. Mix together the butter, lime juice, lime zest, chili powder, salt, and pepper.

3. Divide the butter mixture evenly between the six ears of corn and spread it over the ears of corn. Wrap them tightly with the foil so they don't leak.

4. Place the foil wrapped ears of corn into the crock. Cover and cook on Low for 4 hours.

Simple Salted Carrots

Hope Comerford
Clinton Township, MI

Makes 4 servings
Prep. Time: 5 minutes ❧ Cooking Time: 2 minutes ❧
Setting: Manual then Sauté ❧ Pressure: High ❧ Release: Manual

1-lb. pkg. baby carrots

1 cup water

1 Tbsp. unsalted butter

sea salt to taste

1. Combine the carrots and water in the inner pot of the Instant Pot.

2. Seal the lid and make sure the vent is on sealing. Select Manual for 2 minutes.

3. When cooking time is done, release the pressure manually then pour the carrots into a strainer.

4. Wipe the inner pot dry. Select the Sauté function and add the butter.

5. When the butter is melted, add the carrots back into the inner pot and sauté them until they are coated well with the butter.

6. Remove the carrots and sprinkle them with the sea salt to taste before serving.

Brown Sugar Glazed Carrots

Instant Pot

Michele Ruvola
Vestal, NY

Makes 10 servings
Prep. Time: 5 minutes ⚜ Cooking Time: 4 minutes ⚜
Setting: Steam ⚜ Pressure: High ⚜ Release: Manual

32-oz. bag of baby carrots
½ cup vegetable broth
½ cup brown sugar
4 Tbsp. butter
½ Tbsp. salt

1. Place all ingredients in inner pot of the Instant Pot.

2. Secure the lid, turn valve to sealing, and set timer for 4 minutes on Manual at high pressure.

3. When cooking time is up, perform a quick release to release pressure.

4. Stir carrots, then serve.

Doris's Broccoli and Cauliflower with Cheese

Doris G. Herr
Manheim, PA

Makes 8 servings
Prep. Time: 5 minutes   ⚬   Cooking Time: 1½–3 hours   ⚬   Ideal slow-cooker size: 3-qt.

1 lb. frozen chopped cauliflower

2 (10-oz.) pkgs. frozen chopped broccoli

½ cup water

2 cups shredded cheddar cheese

1. Place cauliflower and broccoli in slow cooker.

2. Add water. Top with cheese.

3. Cook on Low 1½–3 hours, depending upon how crunchy or soft you want the vegetables.

Fresh Green Beans

Lizzie Ann Yoder
Hartville, OH

Makes 6–8 servings
Prep. Time: 20 minutes ☙ Cooking Time: 6–24 hours ☙ Ideal slow-cooker size: 4- to 5-qt.

¼ lb. ham pieces, or browned bacon pieces

2 lbs. fresh green beans, washed and cut into pieces, or frenched

3–4 cups water

1 scant tsp. salt

1. Place all ingredients in slow cooker. Mix together well.

2. Cover and cook on High 6–10 hours, or on Low 10–24 hours, or until beans are done to your liking.

Green Beans with Dill

Rebecca Leichty
Harrisonburg, VA

Makes 8 servings
Prep. Time: 5 minutes ❧ *Cooking Time: 3–4 hours* ❧ *Ideal slow-cooker size: 3½- or 4-qt.*

2 qts. fresh cut green beans, or 4 (14½-oz.) cans cut green beans

2 tsp. beef bouillon granules

½ tsp. dill seed

¼ cup water

1. Spray slow cooker with fat-free cooking spray.

2. Add all ingredients and mix well.

3. Cook on High 3–4 hours, or until beans are done to your liking.

Barbecued Green Beans

Sharon Timpe
Jackson, WI

Ruth E. Martin
Loysville, PA

Makes 10–12 servings
Prep. Time: 15 minutes   ❧   Cooking Time: 3–4 hours   ❧   Ideal slow-cooker size: 4-qt.

3 (14½-oz.) cans cut green beans
(drain 2 cans completely; reserve liquid
from 1 can)

1 small onion, diced

1 cup ketchup

¾ cup brown sugar

4 strips bacon, cooked crisp and
crumbled

1. Combine green beans, diced onion, ketchup, and brown sugar in your slow cooker.

2. Add ⅓ cup of reserved bean liquid. Mix gently.

3. Cover and cook on Low 3–4 hours, until beans are tender and heated through. Stir at the end of 2 hours of cooking, if you're home.

4. Pour in a little reserved bean juice if the sauce thickens more than you like.

5. Sprinkle bacon over beans just before serving.

Tip:

Use 1½ lbs. fresh green beans instead of canned beans. When using fresh beans, you'll need to increase the cooking time to 5–6 hours on Low, depending upon how soft or crunchy you like your beans.

Perfect Sweet Potatoes

Instant Pot

Brittney Horst
Lititz, PA

Makes 4–6 servings
Prep. Time: 5 minutes & Cooking Time: 15 minutes &
Setting: Manual & Pressure: High & Release: Natural

4–6 medium sweet potatoes

1 cup water

1. Scrub skin of sweet potatoes with a brush until clean. Pour water into inner pot of the Instant Pot. Place steamer basket in the bottom of the inner pot. Place sweet potatoes on top of steamer basket.

2. Secure the lid and turn valve to seal.

3. Select the Manual mode and set to Pressure Cook on high for 15 minutes.

4. Allow pressure to release naturally (about 10 minutes).

5. Once the pressure valve lowers, remove lid and serve immediately.

Tip:

Super large sweet potatoes need more than 15 minutes! I tried one mega sweet potato and it was not cooked in the center. Maybe 20 minutes will do.

Baked Potatoes

Mary Jane Musser
Manheim, PA

Makes 6 servings
Prep. Time: 5–10 minutes ☙ *Cooking Time: 3–8 hours* ☙ *Ideal slow-cooker size: 4- or 5-qt.*

6 medium-sized baking potatoes

nonfat cooking spray

1. Prick potatoes with fork.

2. Coat each potato with cooking spray. Place potatoes in slow cooker.

3. Cover. Cook on Low 6–8 hours or on High 3–4 hours, or until potatoes are tender, but not browned.

Potatoes with Parsley

Instant Pot

Colleen Heatwole
Burton, MI

Makes 4 servings
Prep. Time: 10 minutes ❧ Cooking Time: 5 minutes ❧
Setting: Sauté then Manual ❧ Pressure: High ❧ Release: Manual

3 Tbsp. butter, *divided*

2 lbs. medium red potatoes (about 2 oz. each), halved lengthwise

1 clove garlic, minced

½ tsp. salt

½ cup chicken broth

2 Tbsp. chopped fresh parsley

1. Place 1 Tbsp. butter in the inner pot of the Instant Pot and select Sauté.

2. After butter is melted, add potatoes, garlic, and salt, stirring well.

3. Sauté 4 minutes, stirring frequently.

4. Add chicken broth and stir well.

5. Seal lid, make sure vent is on sealing, then select Manual for 5 minutes on high pressure.

6. When cooking time is up, manually release the pressure.

7. Strain potatoes, toss with remaining 2 Tbsp. butter and chopped parsley, and serve immediately.

Mashed Potatoes

Instant Pot

Colleen Heatwole
Burton, MI

Makes 3–4 servings
Prep. Time: 10 minutes   &   Cooking Time: 5 minutes   &
Setting: Manual   &   Pressure: High   &   Release: Manual

I cup water

6 medium potatoes, peeled and quartered

2 Tbsp. unsalted butter

½–¾ cup milk, warmed

salt and pepper to taste

1. Add 1 cup water to the inner pot of the Instant Pot. Put the steamer basket in the pot and place potatoes in the basket.

2. Seal the lid and make sure vent is at sealing. Using Manual mode, select 5 minutes cook time high pressure.

3. When cook time ends, do a manual release. Use a fork to test potatoes. If needed, relock lid and cook at high pressure a few minutes more.

4. Transfer potatoes to large mixing bowl. Mash using hand mixer, stirring in butter. Gradually add warmed milk. Season with salt and pepper to taste.

Note from the cook:

A few lumps are okay . . . that lets you know they are real potatoes. Some people prefer a ricer to a hand mixer for perfect, lump-free mashed potatoes. I used to do it that way, but my family is fine with hand-mixer mashed potatoes.

Garlicky Potatoes

Donna Lantgen
Rapid City, SD

Makes 6 servings
Prep. Time: 15–20 minutes ⚜ *Cooking Time: 5–6 hours* ⚜ *Ideal slow-cooker size: 3½-qt.*

6 potatoes, peeled and cubed

6 cloves garlic, minced

¼ cup dried minced onion, or one medium onion, chopped

2 Tbsp. olive oil

1. Combine all ingredients in slow cooker.

2. Cook on Low 5–6 hours, or until potatoes are soft but not turning brown.

Creamy Red Potatoes

J. E. Barthold
Bethlehem, PA

Makes 4–6 servings
Prep. Time: 10 minutes ♣ *Cooking Time: 8 hours* ♣ *Ideal slow-cooker size: 4-qt.*

2 lbs. small red potatoes, quartered

8-oz. pkg. cream cheese, softened

10¾-oz. can cream of potato soup

1 envelope dry ranch salad dressing mix

1. Place potatoes in slow cooker.

2. Beat together cream cheese, soup, and salad dressing mix. Stir into potatoes.

3. Cover. Cook on Low 8 hours, or until potatoes are tender.

Pizza Potatoes

Margaret Wenger Johnson
Keezletown, VA

Makes 4–6 servings
Prep. Time: 15 minutes ⚜ *Cooking Time: 6–10 hours* ⚜ *Ideal slow-cooker size: 4-qt.*

6 medium potatoes, sliced

1 large onion, thinly sliced

2 Tbsp. olive oil

2 cups grated mozzarella cheese

2 oz. sliced pepperoni

1 tsp. salt

8-oz. can pizza sauce

1. If you have access to a stove top, sauté potato and onion slices in oil in skillet until onions appear transparent. Drain well. If not, skip to Step 2 and omit the oil.

2. In slow cooker, combine potatoes, onions, cheese, pepperoni, and salt.

3. Pour pizza sauce over top.

4. Cover. Cook on Low 6–10 hours, or until potatoes are soft.

Slow-Cooker Cheese Potatoes

Berenice M. Wagner
Dodge City, KS

Marilyn Yoder
Archbold, OH

Makes 6 servings
Prep. Time: 5 minutes   ❧   Cooking Time: 7 hours   ❧   Ideal slow-cooker size: 4-qt.

2-lb. pkg. frozen hash browns
10¾-oz. can cream of potato soup
10¾-oz. can cream of mushroom soup
8 oz. (2 cups) shredded cheddar cheese
1 cup grated Parmesan cheese
1 pint sour cream

1. Mix together all ingredients in slow cooker.

2. Cover. Cook on Low 7 hours.

Lynn's Jazzy Baked Beans

Lynn Houbeck
Chesterfield, MI

Makes 8 servings
Prep. Time: 10 minutes ❧ Cooking Time: 4 hours ❧ Ideal slow-cooker size: 4-qt.

28-oz. can Bush's Original Baked Beans
15-oz. can kidney beans, drained
15-oz. can butter beans, drained
1 small onion, chopped
½ lb. bacon, cooked and chopped
½ cup brown sugar

1. Mix all ingredients together in the crock.

2. Cover and cook on High for 4 hours, or until thickened.

Baked Navy Beans

Colleen Heatwole
Burton, MI

Makes 8 servings
Prep. Time: 15 minutes & Cooking Time: 25 minutes &
Setting: Manual then Slow Cook & Pressure: High & Release: Natural then Manual

10 oz. (about 8 slices) thick sliced bacon, cut into ½-inch pieces

1 large onion, chopped

2½ cups water

½ cup molasses

½ cup ketchup

¼ cup brown sugar

1 tsp. dry mustard

½ tsp. salt

¼ tsp. ground black pepper

1 lb. navy beans, cleaned, rinsed, soaked overnight in 8 cups water mixed with 1 Tbsp. salt

1. Using Sauté function, cook bacon in the inner pot of the Instant Pot until crisp, about 5 minutes, stirring frequently.

2. Remove bacon using slotted spoon and place on plate lined with paper towels.

3. Cook the onion in bacon fat left in the inner pot until tender, about 3 minutes, stirring frequently and scraping up the brown bits on the bottom of the pot as the onion cooks.

4. Add water, molasses, ketchup, brown sugar, dry mustard, salt, and pepper and stir to combine. Stir in the soaked beans.

5. Secure lid and make sure vent is on sealing. Select Manual at high pressure and set for 25 minutes cook time.

6. When timer on pot beeps, let pressure release naturally for 10 minutes, then do a quick release for the remaining pressure.

7. Discard any beans floating on top. Check beans for tenderness. If not done, pressure cook a few minutes longer.

8. Stir in cooked bacon. Using Slow Cook function, cook beans uncovered until sauce is desired consistency. Stir frequently to avoid burning the sauce.

Barbecued Baked Beans

Mary Ann Bowman
East Earl, PA

Makes 8–10 servings
Prep. Time: 10 minutes ❧ *Cooking Time: 3–4 hours* ❧ *Ideal slow-cooker size: 4-qt.*

2 (16-oz.) cans baked beans, your
choice of variety

2 (15-oz.) cans kidney or pinto beans,
or one of each, drained

½ cup brown sugar

1 cup ketchup

1 onion, chopped

1. Combine all ingredients in slow cooker. Mix well.

2. Cover and cook on Low 3–4 hours, or until heated through.

Perfect White Rice

Hope Comerford
Clinton Township, MI

Makes 4 servings
Prep. Time: 2 minutes   ⚶   Cooking Time: 8 minutes   ⚶
Setting: Rice   ⚶   Pressure: High   ⚶   Release: Natural then Manual

1 cup uncooked white rice

1 tsp. grapeseed, olive, or coconut oil

1 cup water

pinch of salt

1. Rinse rice under cold running water until the water runs clear, then pour into the inner pot.

2. Add oil, water, and salt to the inner pot.

3. Lock the lid and set the steam valve to its sealing position. Select the Rice button and set to cook for 8 minutes.

4. Allow the pressure to release naturally for 10 minutes and then release any remaining pressure manually.

5. Fluff the rice with a fork and serve.

Rice Guiso

Instant Pot

Cynthia Hockman-Chupp
Canby, OR

Makes 3–6 servings
Prep. Time: 5 minutes ⚘ *Cooking Time: 15 minutes* ⚘
Setting: Rice ⚘ *Pressure: High* ⚘ *Release: Natural or Manual*

1 Tbsp. oil (I prefer coconut)

1 onion, chopped

1 cup rice

1 tsp. salt

⅛ tsp. pepper

¼–½ cup chopped bell pepper, any color (or a variety of colors!)

1–1⅛ cups water

2 Tbsp. tomato paste

1. Place all ingredients in inner pot of the Instant Pot. Stir.

2. Secure the lid and make sure vent is at sealing. Push Rice button and set for 15 minutes. Allow to cook.

3. Use manual release for a final product that is more moist; natural release for a slightly drier rice. I prefer natural release for this rice.

Best Brown Rice

Instant Pot

Colleen Heatwole
Burton, MI

Makes 6–12 servings
Prep. Time: 5 minutes ⚬ Cooking Time: 22 minutes ⚬
Setting: Manual ⚬ Pressure: High ⚬ Release: Natural then Manual

2 cups brown rice

2½ cups water

1. Rinse brown rice in a fine mesh strainer.

2. Add rice and water to the inner pot of the Instant Pot.

3. Secure the lid and make sure vent is on sealing.

4. Use Manual setting and select 22 minutes cooking time on high pressure.

5. When cooking time is done, let the pressure release naturally for 10 minutes, then press Cancel and manually release any remaining pressure.

Desserts & Beverages

Desserts

Dessert Fondue

Sara Kinsinger
Stuarts Draft, VA

Bonita Ensenberger
Albuquerque, NM

Makes about 3 cups

Prep. Time: 10–15 minutes & *Cooking Time: 2 hours* & *Ideal slow-cooker size: 4-qt.*

I Tbsp. butter

16 (1-oz.) candy bars, half milk chocolate; half semi-sweet chocolate, broken

30 large marshmallows

⅓ cup milk

I cup whipping cream

1. Grease slow cooker with butter. Turn to High for 10 minutes.

2. Meanwhile, mix broken candy bars, marshmallows, and milk together in a bowl.

3. Put candy/milk mixture into slow cooker.

4. Cover and cook on Low for 30 minutes. Stir. Cover and cook another 30 minutes. Stir.

5. Gradually stir in whipping cream. Cover and cook on Low another hour.

Serving suggestion:
Serve the fondue warm from the cooker with pieces of pound cake, angel-food cake, bananas, and pretzels for dipping.

Brownies with Nuts

Dorothy VanDeest
Memphis, TN

Makes 24 brownies
Prep. Time: 10–15 minutes & Cooking Time: 3 hours & Ideal slow-cooker size: 5-qt.

4 Tbsp. (½ stick) butter, melted

I cup chopped nuts, *divided*

23-oz. pkg. brownie mix

1. Pour melted butter into a baking insert designed to fit into your slow cooker. Swirl butter around to grease sides of insert.

2. Sprinkle butter with half the nuts.

3. In a bowl, mix brownies according to package directions. Spoon half the batter into the baking insert, trying to cover the nuts evenly.

4. Add remaining half of nuts. Spoon in remaining batter.

5. Place insert in slow cooker. Cover insert with 8 paper towels.

6. Cover cooker. Cook on High 3 hours. Do not check or remove cover until last hour of cooking. Then insert toothpick into center of brownies. If it comes out clean, the brownies are finished. If it doesn't, continue cooking another 15 minutes. Check again. Repeat until pick comes out clean.

7. When finished cooking, uncover cooker and baking insert. Let brownies stand 5 minutes.

8. Invert insert onto serving plate. Cut brownies with a plastic knife (so the crumbs don't drag). Serve warm.

Dark Chocolate Lava Cake

Hope Comerford
Clinton Township, MI

Makes 8 servings
Prep. Time: 5–10 minutes
Cook Time: 2–3 hours ⚓ *Ideal slow-cooker size: 4-qt.*

5 eggs

1 cup dark cocoa powder

⅔ cup maple syrup

⅔ cup dark chocolate, chopped into very fine pieces or shaved

1. Whisk the eggs together in a bowl and then slowly whisk in the remaining ingredients.

2. Spray the crock with nonstick spray.

3. Pour the egg/chocolate mixture into the crock.

4. Cover and cook on Low for 2–3 hours with some folded paper towels under the lid to collect condensation. It is done when the middle is set and bounces back up when touched.

Dump Cake

Instant Pot

Janie Steele
Moore, OK

Makes 8–10 servings
Prep. Time: 10 minutes ♣ Cooking Time: 12 minutes ♣
Setting: Manual ♣ Pressure: High ♣ Release: Manual

6 Tbsp. butter

1 box cake mix (I used spice)

2 (20-oz.) cans pie filling (I used apple)

1. Mix butter and dry cake mix in bowl. It will be clumpy.

2. Pour pie filling in the inner pot of the Instant Pot.

3. Pour the dry mix over top.

4. Secure lid and make sure vent is at sealing. Cook for 12 minutes on Manual mode at high pressure.

5. Release pressure manually when cook time is up and remove lid to prevent condensation from getting into cake.

6. Let stand 5–10 minutes.

Serving suggestion:
Serve with ice cream.

Chocolate Peanut Butter Swirl Dump Cake

Hope Comerford
Clinton Township, MI

Makes 8–10 servings
Prep. Time: 10 minutes ❧ *Cooking Time: 2–4 hours* ❧ *Ideal slow-cooker size: 3½- to 4-qt.*

15¼-oz. box chocolate cake mix

3.4-oz. box butterscotch instant pudding

1¾ cups milk

4 (1½-oz.) pkgs. Reese's Peanut Butter Cups, chopped

¼ cup peanut butter

1. Spray crock with nonstick spray.

2. In a bowl, mix together the first three ingredients, then dump them into the crock.

3. Sprinkle chopped Reese's over the top of the batter, then swirl the peanut butter in with a spoon.

4. Cover and cook on Low for 2–4 hours.

Chocolate Cherry Dessert

Janie Steele
Moore, OK

Makes 6 servings
Prep. Time: 5 minutes ⚜ *Cooking Time: 3 hours* ⚜ *Ideal slow-cooker size: 3-qt.*

12½-oz. can cherry pie filling
1 box chocolate cake mix
4 Tbsp. (½ stick) butter, melted

1. Pour pie filling in greased slow cooker.

2. Mix dry cake mix and melted butter together. Sprinkle this over pie filling.

3. Cover and cook on Low for 3 hours.

Serving Suggestion:
Serve with ice cream or whipped topping.

Funfetti Dump Cake

Hope Comerford
Clinton Township, MI

Makes 8–10 servings
Prep. Time: 5 minutes & Cooking Time: 3–5 hours & Ideal slow-cooker size: 3½- or 4-qt.

15¼-oz. box Funfetti cake mix

3.4-oz. box vanilla instant pudding

2 cups milk

½ cup rainbow sprinkles

1. Spray crock with nonstick spray.

2. In a bowl, mix together the first three ingredients. Once blended, stir in the sprinkles, then dump in the crock.

3. Cover and cook on Low for 3–5 hours.

Lemon Dump Cake

Janie Steele
Moore, OK

Makes 6 servings
Prep. Time: 10 minutes ❧ Cooking Time: 4 hours ❧ Ideal slow-cooker size: 6-qt.

2 (15¾-oz.) cans lemon pie filling
15¼-oz. box lemon cake mix
8 Tbsp. (1 stick) butter, melted

1. Pour pie filling in greased slow cooker.

2. Mix cake mix and melted butter together in a bowl.

3. Sprinkle cake mixture over pie filling.

4. Cook 4 hours on Low.

Serving suggestion:
Serve with whipped topping.

Simply Apple Dump Cake

Hope Comerford
Clinton Township, MI

Make 10–12 servings
Prep. Time: 10 minutes ❧ *Cooking Time: 3–5 hours* ❧ *Ideal slow-cooker size: 3½- or 4-qt.*

21-oz. can apple pie filling

18¾-oz. box yellow cake mix

8 Tbsp. (1 stick) butter, melted

1. Spray crock with nonstick spray.

2. Dump apple pie filling into crock.

3. In a bowl, mix together the yellow cake mix and melted butter. Spoon this into the crock.

4. Cover and cook on Low for 3–5 hours.

Blackberry Dump Cake

Hope Comerford
Clinton Township, MI

Makes 8–10 servings
Prep. Time: 15 minutes ⚬ *Cooking Time: 3–5 hours* ⚬ *Ideal slow-cooker size: 3½- or 4-qt.*

15-oz. box yellow cake mix

3-oz. box blackberry gelatin mix

8 Tbsp. (1 stick) butter, melted

1 cup water

4 cups blackberries

1. Spray crock with nonstick spray.

2. In a bowl, mix the first four ingredients together. Once blended, gently fold in the blackberries, then dump the batter into the crock.

3. Cover and cook on Low for 3–5 hours.

Cherry Dump Dessert

Anita Troyer
Fairview, MI

Charlotte Shaffer
East Earl, PA

Makes 8 servings
Prep. Time: 10 minutes ⚬ *Cooking Time: 2 hours* ⚬ *Ideal slow-cooker size: 4-qt.*

2 (21-oz.) cans cherry pie filling
18-oz. box white cake mix
12 Tbsp. (1½ sticks) butter, melted

1. Place the cherry filling into crock.

2. Pour cake mix onto cherries.

3. Drizzle melted butter over top, taking care to cover as much surface as possible.

4. Cover and cook on High for 2 hours.

Serving suggestion:
May serve as is or with milk or ice cream.

Apple Caramel Pie

Sue Hamilton
Minooka, IL

Makes 8–10 servings
Prep. Time: 5 minutes & Cooking Time: 3 hours & Ideal slow-cooker size: 4- to 5-qt.

2-crust pkg. refrigerated pie dough
2 (22-oz.) cans apple pie filling
1 tsp. cinnamon
12 caramel candies

1. Press one crust into half the bottom of a cold slow cooker, and an inch or so up half its interior side. Press second crust into other half of the crock, overlapping the first crust by ¼ inch. Press remainder of second crust an inch or so up the remaining side of the cooker. Press seams flat where two crusts meet.

2. Cover. Cook on High 1½ hours.

3. In a bowl, mix together pie filling, cinnamon, and caramels.

4. Pour mixture into hot crust.

5. Cover. Cook on High an additional 1½ hours.

Cherry Cobbler

Michele Ruvola
Selden, NY

Makes 6–8 servings
Prep. Time: 5 minutes ❧ *Cooking Time: 2½–5½ hours* ❧ *Ideal slow-cooker size: 3-qt.*

16-oz. can cherry pie filling

1¾ cups dry cake mix of your choice

1 egg

3 Tbsp. evaporated milk

½ tsp. cinnamon

1. Lightly spray the slow cooker with nonstick cooking spray.

2. Place pie filling in slow cooker and cook on High 30 minutes.

3. Meanwhile, mix together remaining ingredients in bowl until crumbly. Spoon onto hot pie filling.

4. Cover and cook on Low 2–5 hours, or until a toothpick inserted into center of topping comes out dry.

5. Serve warm or cooled.

Quick Yummy Peaches

Willard E. Roth
Elkhart, IN

Makes 6 servings
Prep. Time: 10 minutes & Cooking Time: 5 hours & Ideal slow-cooker size: 3½-qt.

⅓ cup buttermilk baking mix
⅔ cup dry quick oats
½ cup brown sugar
1 tsp. cinnamon
4 cups sliced peaches (canned or fresh)
½ cup peach juice, or water

1. Mix baking mix, oats, brown sugar, and cinnamon together in greased slow cooker.

2. Stir in peaches and peach juice.

3. Cook on Low for at least 5 hours. (If you like a drier cobbler, remove lid for last 15–30 minutes of cooking.)

Serving suggestion:

Serve with frozen yogurt or ice cream.

Baked Apples

Instant Pot

Judy Gascho
Woodburn, OR

Makes 6 servings
Prep. Time: 15 minutes ⚬ *Cooking Time: 9 minutes* ⚬
Setting: Manual ⚬ *Pressure: High* ⚬ *Release: Natural then Manual*

6 medium apples, cored

1 cup apple juice or cider

¼ cup raisins or dried cranberries

½ cup brown sugar

1 tsp. cinnamon

1. Put the apples into the inner pot of the Instant Pot.

2. Pour in the apple juice or cider. Sprinkle the raisins, sugar, and cinnamon over the apples.

3. Close and lock the lid and be sure the steam vent is in the sealing position.

4. Cook for 9 minutes on Manual mode at high pressure.

5. When time is up, unplug and turn off the pressure cooker. Let pressure release naturally for 15 minutes, then manually release any remaining pressure.

6. Take off lid and remove apples to individual small bowls, adding cooking liquid to each.

Marshmallow Applesauce Dessert

Marla Folkerts
Holland, OH

Makes 6–8 servings
Prep. Time: 5 minutes ⚬ Cooking Time: 1½–4 hours ⚬ Ideal slow-cooker size: 4-qt.

4 cups applesauce
¼ tsp. allspice
½ tsp. cinnamon
2 cups mini-marshmallows

1. Spray slow cooker with nonfat cooking spray.

2. In the cooker, mix applesauce, allspice, and cinnamon together.

3. Sprinkle marshmallows on top.

4. Cook on Low 3–4 hours, or on High 1½–2 hours.

Serving suggestion:
Serve warm from slow cooker.

Note:
This is delicious over ice cream and cake!
We've even used it as a fondue for fruit!

Bananas Foster

Hope Comerford
Clinton Township, MI

Makes 6 servings
Prep. Time: 5–10 minutes ❧ *Cooking Time: 1½–2 hours* ❧ *Ideal slow-cooker size: 4-qt.*

I Tbsp. melted coconut oil

3 Tbsp. raw honey

3 Tbsp. fresh lemon juice

¼ tsp. cinnamon

dash nutmeg

5 bananas (not green, but just yellow),
sliced into ½-inch-thick slices

1. Combine the first 5 ingredients in the crock.

2. Add the bananas and stir to coat them evenly.

3. Cover and cook on Low for 1½–2 hours.

Tapioca Salad

Karen Ashworth
Duenweg, MO

Makes 10–12 servings
Prep. Time: 10 minutes   &   Cooking Time: 3 hours   &   Ideal slow-cooker size: 4½-qt.

10 Tbsp. large pearl tapioca
½ cup sugar or to taste
dash salt
4 cups water
1 cup grapes, cut in half
1 cup crushed pineapple
1 cup whipped cream

1. Mix together tapioca, sugar, salt, and water in slow cooker.

2. Cook on High 3 hours, or until tapioca pearls are almost translucent.

3. Cool thoroughly in refrigerator.

4. Stir in remaining ingredients.

Serving suggestion:
Serve cold.

Variation:
Add 1 small can mandarin oranges, drained, when adding rest of fruit.

Beverages

Creamy Hot Chocolate

Deborah Heatwole
Waynesboro, GA

Makes 8 servings
Prep. Time: 15 minutes ❧ Cooking Time: 2–4 hours ❧ Ideal slow-cooker size: 3-qt.

½ cup dry baking cocoa

14-oz. can sweetened condensed milk

⅛ tsp. salt

7½ cups water

1½ tsp. vanilla extract

24 or more mini marshmallows,
optional

1. In slow cooker, combine dry cocoa, milk, and salt. Stir until smooth. Add water gradually, stirring until smooth.

2. Cover and cook on High 2 hours, or on Low 4 hours, or until very hot.

3. Just before serving, stir in vanilla.

4. Top each serving with 3 or more marshmallows, if you wish.

Tips:

1. To speed things up, heat the water before adding it to the chocolate mixture.

2. Keep hot chocolate warm on Low up to 4 hours in the slow cooker.

3. Add a mocha flavor by stirring in instant coffee in Step 3.

Dark Chocolate Peanut Butter Cocoa

Hope Comerford
Clinton Township, MI

Makes 10–12 servings
Prep. Time: 5 minutes ♣ Cook Time: 5–6 hours ♣ Ideal slow-cooker size: 3- or 4-qt.

8 cups almond milk

½ cup powdered peanut butter

¼ cup turbinado sugar

12 oz. dark chocolate, broken into pieces

1 Tbsp. vanilla extract

1. Combine almond milk, powdered peanut butter, and turbinado sugar in crock.

2. Cover and cook on Low for 5–6 hours.

3. Stir in chocolate and vanilla until chocolate is melted, then serve.

Hot Mint Malt

Clarice Williams
Fairbank, IA

Makes 6 servings
Prep. Time: 5 minutes ❦ *Cooking Time: 2–3 hours* ❦ *Ideal slow-cooker size: 2- to 3-qt.*

6 chocolate-covered cream-filled mint patties

5 cups milk

½ cup chocolate malted milk powder

1 tsp. vanilla extract

whipping cream, whipped stiff

1. In slow cooker, combine mint patties with milk, malted milk powder, and vanilla.

2. Heat on Low 2–3 hours. If you're able, stir occasionally to help melt the patties.

3. When the drink is thoroughly heated, beat with rotary beater until frothy.

4. Pour into cups and top with whipped cream.

Spiced Coffee

Esther Burkholder
Millerstown, PA

Makes 8 servings
Prep. Time: 10 minutes & Cooking Time: 3 hours & Ideal slow-cooker size: 3-qt.

8 cups brewed coffee
⅓ cup sugar
¼ cup chocolate syrup
4 (3-inch-long) cinnamon sticks
1½ tsp. whole cloves

1. Pour coffee into slow cooker. Stir in sugar and chocolate syrup.

2. Place cinnamon sticks and whole cloves on a piece of cheesecloth. Tie with string to create a bag. Submerge in slow cooker.

3. Cover and cook on Low 3 hours, or until coffee is very hot. Remove cheesecloth bag.

4. Turn to Low and serve warm from cooker.

Hot Apple Cider

Jeannine Janzen
Elbing, KS

Makes 4 servings
Prep. Time: 5 minutes ⚖ *Cooking Time: 2–3 hours* ⚖ *Ideal slow-cooker size: 3-qt.*

1 qt. apple cider
⅛ tsp. nutmeg
½ cup red cinnamon hearts

1. Combine all ingredients in slow cooker.

2. Cover and cook on High 2–3 hours, or until very hot. If you're at home and available, stir the cider occasionally to help dissolve the red candy.

3. Serve warm from the slow cooker.

Hot Mulled Cider

Phyllis Attig
Reynolds, IL

Jean Butzer
Batavia, NY

Doris G. Herr
Manheim, PA

Mary E. Martin
Goshen, IN

Leona Miller
Millersburg, OH

Marjora Miller
Archbold, OH

Janet L. Roggie
Lowville, NY

Shirley Sears
Tiskilwa, IL

Charlotte Shaffer
East Earl, PA

Berenice M. Wagner
Dodge City, KS

Connie B. Weaver
Bethlehem, PA

Maryann Westerberg
Rosamond, CA

Carole Whaling
New Tripoli, PA

Makes 8 1-cup servings

Prep. Time: 5 minutes ❧ *Cooking Time: 2–8 hours* ❧ *Ideal slow-cooker size: 3½-qt.*

¼–½ cup brown sugar
2 qts. apple cider
1 tsp. whole allspice
1½ tsp. whole cloves
2 cinnamon sticks
2 oranges, sliced, with peels on

1. Combine brown sugar and cider in slow cooker.

2. Put spices in tea strainer or tie in cheesecloth. Add to slow cooker. Stir in orange slices.

3. Cover and simmer on Low 2–8 hours.

Variation:

Add a dash of ground nutmeg and salt.

—Marsha Sabus, Fallbrook, CA

Citrus Cider

Valerie Drobel
Carlisle, PA

Makes 8–10 servings
Prep. Time: 10 minutes ⚸ Cooking Time: 2–5 hours ⚸ Ideal slow-cooker size: 3- to 5-qt.

2 qts. apple cider
½ cup packed brown sugar
2 (4-inch-long) cinnamon sticks
1 tsp. whole cloves
1 orange or lemon, sliced

1. Pour cider into slow cooker. Stir in brown sugar.

2. Place cinnamon sticks and cloves in cheesecloth and tie with string to form a bag. Float in slow cooker.

3. Add fruit slices on top.

4. Cover and cook on Low 2–5 hours. Remove spice bag. Stir before serving.

Variations:

1. Add ⅓ tsp. ground ginger to Step 1.
   —Christie Anne Detamore-Hunsberger,
   Harrisonburg, VA

2. Add 1 tsp. whole allspice to the cheesecloth bag in Step 2.
   —Mary Stauffer, Ephrata, PA

3. Eliminate the brown sugar for a less sweet beverage.
   —Pauline Morrison, St. Marys, ON

Spicy Hot Cider

Michelle High
Fredericksburg, PA

Makes 16 servings
Prep. Time: 5 minutes   Cooking Time: 3 hours   Ideal slow-cooker size: 5-qt.

1 gallon apple cider
4 cinnamon sticks
2 Tbsp. ground allspice
¼–½ cup brown sugar

1. Combine first three ingredients in slow cooker. Add ¼ cup brown sugar. Stir to dissolve. If you'd like the cider to be sweeter, add more, up to ½ cup total.

2. Cover and cook on Low 3 hours.

3. Serve warm from the cooker.

Spiced Cranberry Cider

Esther Burkholder
Millerstown, PA

Makes 7 servings
Prep. Time: 5–10 minutes ☙ *Cooking Time: 3–5 hours* ☙ *Ideal slow-cooker size: 3-qt.*

1 qt. apple cider
3 cups cranberry juice cocktail
3 Tbsp. brown sugar
2 (3-inch-long) cinnamon sticks
¾ tsp. whole cloves
½ lemon, thinly sliced, *optional*

1. Pour apple cider and cranberry juice into slow cooker.

2. Stir in brown sugar.

3. Put spices on a piece of cheesecloth. Tie with a string to create a bag. Place in slow cooker.

4. Stir in lemon slices if you wish.

5. Cover and cook on Low 3–5 hours, or until cider is very hot. If you're able, stir occasionally to be sure brown sugar is dissolving.

6. Remove spice bag, and lemon slices if you've included them, before serving warm from the cooker.

Variation:

Instead of whole cloves, substitute 1 tsp. whole allspice.

—Jean Butzer, Batavia, NY

Metric Equivalent Measurements

If you're accustomed to using metric measurements, I don't want you to be inconvenienced by the imperial measurements I use in this book.

Use this handy chart, too, to figure out the size of the slow cooker you'll need for each recipe.

Weight (Dry Ingredients)

1 oz		30 g
4 oz	¼ lb	120 g
8 oz	½ lb	240 g
12 oz	¾ lb	360 g
16 oz	1 lb	480 g
32 oz	2 lb	960 g

Slow Cooker Sizes

1-quart	0.96 l
2-quart	1.92 l
3-quart	2.88 l
4-quart	3.84 l
5-quart	4.80 l
6-quart	5.76 l
7-quart	6.72 l
8-quart	7.68 l

Volume (Liquid Ingredients)

½ tsp.		2 ml
1 tsp.		5 ml
1 Tbsp.	½ fl oz	15 ml
2 Tbsp.	1 fl oz	30 ml
¼ cup	2 fl oz	60 ml
⅓ cup	3 fl oz	80 ml
½ cup	4 fl oz	120 ml
⅔ cup	5 fl oz	160 ml
¾ cup	6 fl oz	180 ml
1 cup	8 fl oz	240 ml
1 pt	16 fl oz	480 ml
1 qt	32 fl oz	960 ml

Length

¼ in	6 mm
½ in	13 mm
¾ in	19 mm
1 in	25 mm
6 in	15 cm
12 in	30 cm

Recipe and Ingredient Index

A

All-Day Pot Roast, 138
Apple Breakfast Cobbler, 33
Apple Caramel Pie, 249
apple cider
  Citrus Cider, 269
  Hot Apple Cider, 267
  Hot Mulled Cider, 268
  Spiced Cranberry Cider, 273
  Spicy Hot Cider, 271
apple pie filling
  Simply Apple Dump Cake, 243
apples
  Baked Apples, 254
  Breakfast Apples, 35
applesauce
  Marshmallow Applesauce Dessert, 255

B

bacon
  Baked Navy Beans, 217
  Canadian
    Kelly's Split Pea Soup, 93
  Lynn's Jazzy Baked Beans, 215
  Mountain Bike Soup, 94
Baked Apples, 254
Baked Navy Beans, 217
Baked Potatoes, 203
Bananas Foster, 257
Barbecued Baked Beans, 219
Barbecued Beef Sandwiches, 149
Barbecued Cocktail Sausages, 51

Barbecued Green Beans, 199
Barbecued Ribs, 175
barbecue sauce
  Barbecued Ribs, 175
  BBQ Pork Sandwiches, 180
  Beef Brisket Barbecue, 148
  Honey Barbecue Pork Chops, 171
  Pulled Pork, 179
  Quickie Barbecued Chicken, 118
  Super Beef Barbecue, 152
  Tender Barbecued Chicken, 117
barley
  Beef Barley Soup, 83
  Mountain Bike Soup, 94
BBQ Pork Sandwiches, 180
beans
  baked
    Barbecued Baked Beans, 219
    Ham and Bean Stew, 99
    Lynn's Jazzy Baked Beans, 215
  Baked Navy Beans, 217
  Barbecued Green Beans, 199
  black
    Beans and Tomato Chili, 109
    Easy Chicken Tortilla Soup, 69
    Versatile Slow-Cooker Chili, 90
  butter
    Lynn's Jazzy Baked Beans, 215
  chili
    Easy Crock Taco Filling, 160
    Extra Easy Chili, 87
    6-Can Soup, 105

garbanzo
    Beans and Tomato Chili, 109
green
    Fresh Green Beans, 195
    Mountain Bike Soup, 94
    Smoked Sausage Stew, 95
Huevos Rancheros in Crock, 23
kidney
    Barbecued Baked Beans, 219
    Beans and Tomato Chili, 109
    Chili with Two Beans, 89
    Lynn's Jazzy Baked Beans, 215
    Santa Fe Soup with Melted Cheese,
      80
    Taco Soup, 77
    Versatile Slow-Cooker Chili, 90
navy
    Baked Navy Beans, 217
pinto
    Barbecued Baked Beans, 219
    Beans and Tomato Chili, 109
    Chili Taco Soup, 79
    Chili with Two Beans, 89
    Taco Soup with Pinto Beans, 78
ranch-style
    Quick Taco Chicken Soup, 67
red
    Turkey Chili, 73
refried
    Southwest Hot Chip Dip, 55
Beans and Tomato Chili, 109
beef
    All-Day Pot Roast, 138
    brisket
     Beef Brisket Barbecue, 148
    chuck roast

Beef Barley Soup, 83
ground, 15
    Chili-Cheese Taco Dip, 56
    Chili with Two Beans, 89
    Easy Beef Tortillas, 161
    Easy Crock Taco Filling, 160
    Easy Hamburgers, 156
    Easy Meatloaf, 153
    Extra Easy Chili, 87
    Ground Beef Vegetable Soup, 81
    Meatloaf, 155
    Santa Fe Soup with Melted Cheese,
      80
    Sloppy Joes, 159
    Southwest Hot Chip Dip, 55
    Taco Soup, 77
    Taco Soup with Pinto Beans, 78
    Versatile Slow-Cooker Chili, 90
roast
    All-Day Pot Roast, 138
    Italian Beef, 145
    Pulled Beef or Pork, 151
    Roast Beef Sandwiches, 146
    Spicy French Dip, 147
    Whole Dinner Roast Beef, 139
    Zesty French Dip, 143
round steak
    Cozy Cabin Casserole, 140
    Slow-Cooked Swiss Steak, 142
    Swiss Steak and Gravy, 141
rump roast
    Super Beef Barbecue, 152
steak
    Barbecued Beef Sandwiches, 149
stew meat
    Chili Taco Soup, 79

Lynn's Easy Stew, 86
Beef Barley Soup, 83
Beef Brisket Barbecue, 148
Beef Stew, 85
beer
    Zesty French Dip, 143
bell pepper
    Rice Guiso, 223
    Slow-Cooked Swiss Steak, 142
Best Brown Rice, 225
Blackberry Dump Cake, 245
Blueberry Fancy, 31
bread
    Beef Brisket Barbecue, 148
    Blueberry Fancy, 31
    Breakfast Sausage Casserole, 19
    Roast Beef Sandwiches, 146
    Sloppy Joes, 159
    Spicy French Dip, 147
    Zesty French Dip, 143
breakfast
    Apple Breakfast Cobbler, 33
    Blueberry Fancy, 31
    Easy Egg and Sausage Puff, 21
    Easy Spinach Quiche, 25
    Huevos Rancheros in Crock, 23
    Layered Breakfast Casserole, 16
    Overnight Oatmeal, 39
    Poached Eggs, 27
    Quick and Easy Instant Pot Cinnamon
        Rolls, 28
    Streusel Cake, 29
Breakfast Apples, 35
Breakfast Bake, 17
Breakfast Oatmeal, 37
Breakfast Sausage Casserole, 19

broccoli
    Cream of Broccoli Soup, 108
    Doris's Broccoli and Cauliflower with
        Cheese, 193
Broccoli Cheese Soup, 107
Brownies with Nuts, 230
Brown Sugar Glazed Carrots, 191
Buffalo Chicken Wing Soup, 71

C
cabbage
    Chicken with Vegetables, 129
cake
    Blackberry Dump Cake, 245
    Chocolate Peanut Butter Swirl Dump
        Cake, 235
    Dark Chocolate Lava Cake, 233
    Dump Cake, 234
    Funfetti Dump Cake, 239
    Lemon Dump Cake, 241
    Simply Apple Dump Cake, 243
    Streusel Cake, 29
candy bars
    Dessert Fondue, 230
caramel candy
    Apple Caramel Pie, 249
Carolina Pot Roast, 169
carrots
    Brown Sugar Glazed Carrots, 191
    Simple Salted Carrots, 189
cauliflower
    Doris's Broccoli and Cauliflower with
        Cheese, 193
cheese
    American
        Cream of Broccoli Soup, 108

Creamy Baked Chicken with
    Stuffing, 131
Breakfast Bake, 17
cheddar
    Breakfast Sausage Casserole, 19
    Chicken Enchiladas, 118
    Doris's Broccoli and Cauliflower with
        Cheese, 193
    Easy Beef Tortillas, 161
    Easy Egg and Sausage Puff, 21
    Slow-Cooker Cheese Potatoes, 214
    Tina's Cheese Dip, 57
Mexican
    Huevos Rancheros in Crock, 23
mozzarella
    Pizza Potatoes, 213
    Tina's Cheese Dip, 57
Parmesan
    Slow-Cooker Cheese Potatoes, 214
pepper jack
    Easy Spinach Quiche, 25
Velveeta
    Chili-Cheese Taco Dip, 56
    Layered Breakfast Casserole, 16
    Santa Fe Soup with Melted Cheese,
        80
    Southwest Hot Chip Dip, 55
    Texas Queso Dip, 59
Cherry Cobbler, 251
Cherry Dump Dessert, 247
cherry pie filling
    Cherry Cobbler, 251
    Cherry Dump Dessert, 247
    Chocolate Cherry Dessert, 237
chicken
    Buffalo Chicken Wing Soup, 71

Chunky Chicken Vegetable Soup, 65
Come-Back-for-More Barbecued
    Chicken, 116
Easy Chicken Tortilla Soup, 69
Easy Creamy Chicken, 122
Greek Chicken Pita Filling, 121
Lemon Pepper Chicken and Veggies, 125
Mary's Chicken and Rice Soup, 66
Quickie Barbecued Chicken, 118
Quick Taco Chicken Soup, 67
Simply Delicious Chicken Breasts, 123
Slow Cooked Honey Garlic Chicken
    Thighs, 115
Slow-Cooker Chicken and Gravy, 127
Sunday Chicken Dinner, 126
Tasty Chicken Soup, 64
Tender Barbecued Chicken, 117
Chicken and Rice Casserole, 133
Chicken and Stuffing, 130
Chicken Enchiladas, 118
Chicken with Broccoli Rice, 135
Chicken with Vegetables, 129
chili
    Beans and Tomato Chili, 109
    Extra Easy Chili, 87
    Turkey Chili, 73
    Versatile Slow-Cooker Chili, 90
Chili Cheese Dip, 53
Chili-Cheese Taco Dip, 56
Chili Lime Corn on the Cob, 187
Chili Nuts, 47
chili sauce
    Sweet 'n Sour Meatballs, 49
Chili Taco Soup, 79
Chili with Two Beans, 89
chocolate

Dark Chocolate Lava Cake, 233
Dark Chocolate Peanut Butter Cocoa,
    263
Chocolate Cherry Dessert, 237
Chocolate Peanut Butter Swirl Dump
    Cake, 235
Chunky Chicken Vegetable Soup, 65
cinnamon rolls
    Quick and Easy Instant Pot Cinnamon
        Rolls, 28
Citrus Cider, 269
cobbler
    Cherry Cobbler, 251
cocoa
    Creamy Hot Chocolate, 262
    Dark Chocolate Lava Cake, 233
    German Chocolate Oatmeal, 41
coconut
    German Chocolate Oatmeal, 41
coffee
    Spiced Coffee, 265
cola
    Barbecued Beef Sandwiches, 149
    Pork Roast, 166
Come-Back-for-More Barbecued Chicken,
    116
corn
    Chicken and Stuffing, 130
    Chili Lime Corn on the Cob, 187
    Chili Taco Soup, 79
    Easy Crock Taco Filling, 160
    Quick Taco Chicken Soup, 67
    Santa Fe Soup with Melted Cheese, 80
    6-Can Soup, 105
    Taco Soup with Pinto Beans, 78
    Turkey Chili, 73

Corn on the Cob, 185
Cozy Cabin Casserole, 140
cranberries
    Baked Apples, 254
cranberry juice
    Spiced Cranberry Cider, 273
cream cheese
    Blueberry Fancy, 31
    Chili Cheese Dip, 53
    Creamy Red Potatoes, 211
    Tina's Cheese Dip, 57
Cream of Broccoli Soup, 108
cream of broccoli soup mix
    Chicken with Broccoli Rice, 135
cream of celery soup
    Chicken and Rice Casserole, 133
    Cozy Cabin Casserole, 140
    Cream of Broccoli Soup, 108
cream of chicken soup
    Buffalo Chicken Wing Soup, 71
    Chicken Enchiladas, 118
    Creamy Baked Chicken with Stuffing,
        131
    Creamy Pork Chops, 170
    Easy Beef Tortillas, 161
    Easy Creamy Chicken, 122
cream of mushroom soup
    Chicken Enchiladas, 118
    Cozy Cabin Casserole, 140
    Cream of Broccoli Soup, 108
    Creamy Sloppy Joes, 157
    Slow-Cooked Swiss Steak, 142
    Slow-Cooker Cheese Potatoes, 214
    Slow-Cooker Chicken and Gravy, 127
    Sunday Chicken Dinner, 126
    Swiss Steak and Gravy, 141

Whole Dinner Roast Beef, 139
cream of potato soup
    Creamy Red Potatoes, 211
    Slow-Cooker Cheese Potatoes, 214
Creamy Baked Chicken with Stuffing, 131
Creamy Hot Chocolate, 262
Creamy Pork Chops, 170
Creamy Red Potatoes, 211
Creamy Sloppy Joes, 157

D
Dark Chocolate Lava Cake, 233
Dark Chocolate Peanut Butter Cocoa, 263
dates
    Breakfast Oatmeal, 37
dessert
    Apple Caramel Pie, 249
    Baked Apples, 254
    Bananas Foster, 257
    Blackberry Dump Cake, 245
    Brownies with Nuts, 230
    Cherry Cobbler, 251
    Cherry Dump Dessert, 247
    Chocolate Cherry Dessert, 237
    Chocolate Peanut Butter Swirl Dump
        Cake, 235
    Creamy Hot Chocolate, 262
    Dark Chocolate Lava Cake, 233
    Dark Chocolate Peanut Butter Cocoa, 263
    Dump Cake, 234
    Funfetti Dump Cake, 239
    Lemon Dump Cake, 241
    Marshmallow Applesauce Dessert, 255
    Quick Yummy Peaches, 253
    Simply Apple Dump Cake, 243
    Streusel Cake, 29

Tapioca Salad, 259
Dessert Fondue, 230
Doris's Broccoli and Cauliflower with
    Cheese, 193
Dump Cake, 234

E
Easy Beef Tortillas, 161
Easy Chicken Tortilla Soup, 69
Easy Creamy Chicken, 122
Easy Crock Taco Filling, 160
Easy Egg and Sausage Puff, 21
Easy Hamburgers, 156
Easy Meatloaf, 153
Easy Spinach Quiche, 25
eggs
    Breakfast Bake, 17
    Breakfast Sausage Casserole, 19
    Easy Spinach Quiche, 25
    Huevos Rancheros in Crock, 23
    Layered Breakfast Casserole, 16
    Poached Eggs, 27
enchiladas
    Chicken Enchiladas, 118
Extra Easy Chili, 87

F
fondue
    Dessert Fondue, 230
French onion soup
    Zesty French Dip, 143
Fresh Green Beans, 195
Funfetti Dump Cake, 239

G
Garlicky Potatoes, 209

German Chocolate Oatmeal, 41
granola
    Apple Breakfast Cobbler, 33
    Breakfast Apples, 35
grape jelly
    Sweet 'n Sour Meatballs, 49
grapes
    Tapioca Salad, 259
Greek Chicken Pita Filling, 121
Green Beans with Dill, 197
green chiles
    Chicken Enchiladas, 118
    Easy Chicken Tortilla Soup, 69
    Shredded Pork, 177
Ground Beef Vegetable Soup, 81

H
ham
    Breakfast Bake, 17
    Fresh Green Beans, 195
    Layered Breakfast Casserole, 16
    Mountain Bike Soup, 94
Ham and Bean Stew, 99
Harry's Vegetable Soup, 102
hash browns
    Ground Beef Vegetable Soup, 81
Hassle-Free Pork Chops, 167
Honey Barbecue Pork Chops, 171
Hot Apple Cider, 267
Hot Dogs, 181
Hot Mint Malt, 264
Hot Mulled Cider, 268
hot sauce
    Buffalo Chicken Wing Soup, 71
Huevos Rancheros in Crock, 23

I
Instant Pot recipes
    Baked Apples, 254
    Baked Navy Beans, 217
    Barbecued Green Beans, 201
    BBQ Pork Sandwiches, 180
    Best Brown Rice, 225
    Brown Sugar Glazed Carrots, 191
    Dump Cake, 234
    Mashed Potatoes, 207
    Perfect White Rice, 221
    Poached Eggs, 27
    Pork Butt Roast, 165
    Potatoes with Parsley, 205
    Pulled Pork, 179
    Quick and Easy Instant Pot Cinnamon
        Rolls, 28
    Rice Guiso, 223
    Slow Cooked Honey Garlic Chicken
        Thighs, 115
    Tender Tasty Ribs, 173
Insta Popcorn, 45
Italian Beef, 145
Italian dressing
    Italian Beef, 145
    Pulled Beef or Pork, 151
    Spicy French Dip, 147

J
jalapeño
    Spicy French Dip, 147

K
Kelly's Split Pea Soup, 93
Kielbasa Soup, 97

L

Layered Breakfast Casserole, 16
Lemon Dump Cake, 241
Lemon Pepper Chicken and
     Veggies, 125
Lynn's Easy Stew, 86
Lynn's Jazzy Baked Beans, 215

M

Marshmallow Applesauce Dessert, 255
marshmallows
     Creamy Hot Chocolate, 262
     Dessert Fondue, 230
Mary's Chicken and Rice Soup, 66
Mashed Potatoes, 207
meatballs
     Sweet 'n Sour Meatballs, 49
meatloaf, 155
     Easy Meatloaf, 153
milk
     Cream of Broccoli Soup, 108
     Sunday Chicken Dinner, 126
mint patties
     Hot Mint Malt, 264
Mountain Bike Soup, 94
mushrooms
     Chicken and Rice Casserole, 133
mushroom soup
     All-Day Pot Roast, 138
     Simply Delicious Chicken Breasts, 123

N

noodles
     Mountain Bike Soup, 94
     Tasty Chicken Soup, 64

O

oats
     Breakfast Oatmeal, 37
     German Chocolate Oatmeal, 41
     Overnight Oatmeal, 39
     Quick Yummy Peaches, 253
onion soup mix
     Chicken and Rice Casserole, 133
     Cozy Cabin Casserole, 140
     Easy Hamburgers, 156
     Ground Beef Vegetable Soup, 81
     Lynn's Easy Stew, 86
     Simply Delicious Chicken Breasts, 123
     Swiss Steak and Gravy, 141
     Whole Dinner Roast Beef, 139
Overnight Oatmeal, 39

P

peaches
     Quick Yummy Peaches, 253
peanut butter
     Chocolate Peanut Butter Swirl Dump
          Cake, 235
     Dark Chocolate Peanut Butter Cocoa,
          263
peanut butter cups
     Chocolate Peanut Butter Swirl Dump
          Cake, 235
peanuts
     Chili Nuts, 47
peas
     Kelly's Split Pea Soup, 93
pepperoni
     Mountain Bike Soup, 94
     Pizza Potatoes, 213
Perfect White Rice, 221

pickles
    Super Beef Barbecue, 152
pineapple
    Tapioca Salad, 259
Pizza Potatoes, 213
Poached Eggs, 27
popcorn
    Insta Popcorn, 45
pork. *See also* ribs
    BBQ Pork Sandwiches, 180
    Carolina Pot Roast, 169
    Creamy Pork Chops, 170
    Hassle-Free Pork Chops, 167
    Honey Barbecue Pork Chops, 171
    Pulled Beef or Pork, 151
    Pulled Pork, 179
    Shredded Pork, 177
Pork Butt Roast, 165
Pork Roast, 166
potatoes
    All-Day Pot Roast, 138
    Baked Potatoes, 203
    Beef Stew, 85
    Creamy Red Potatoes, 211
    Garlicky Potatoes, 209
    Ham and Bean Stew, 99
    hash browns
        Ground Beef Vegetable Soup, 81
    Hassle-Free Pork Chops, 167
    Kielbasa Soup, 97
    Layered Breakfast Casserole, 16
    Lemon Pepper Chicken and Veggies,
        125
    Mashed Potatoes, 207
    Pizza Potatoes, 213
    Potatoes with Parsley, 205

Slow-Cooker Cheese Potatoes, 214
Smoked Sausage Stew, 95
Sunday Chicken Dinner, 126
sweet
    Barbecued Green Beans, 201
    Carolina Pot Roast, 169
    Whole Dinner Roast Beef, 139
Potatoes with Parsley, 205
prosciutto
    Easy Spinach Quiche, 25
pudding
    Funfetti Dump Cake, 239
Pulled Beef or Pork, 151
Pulled Pork, 179

Q
Quick and Easy Instant Pot Cinnamon
    Rolls, 28
Quickie Barbecued Chicken, 118
Quick Taco Chicken Soup, 67
Quick Yummy Peaches, 253

R
raisins
    Breakfast Oatmeal, 37
ranch dressing mix
    Creamy Red Potatoes, 211
    Easy Hamburgers, 156
    Pulled Beef or Pork, 151
    Taco Soup with Pinto Beans, 78
ribs
    Barbecued Ribs, 175
    Tender Tasty Ribs, 173
rice
    Best Brown Rice, 225
    Chicken with Broccoli Rice, 135

Mary's Chicken and Rice Soup, 66
Mountain Bike Soup, 94
Perfect White Rice, 221
Rice Guiso, 223
Rice Guiso, 223
Roast Beef Sandwiches, 146

S

salsa
Chili Cheese Dip, 53
Easy Chicken Tortilla Soup, 69
Huevos Rancheros in Crock, 23
Quick Taco Chicken Soup, 67
Santa Fe Soup with Melted Cheese, 80
sausage
Barbecued Cocktail Sausages, 51
Breakfast Sausage Casserole, 19
Easy Egg and Sausage Puff, 21
kielbasa
Kielbasa Soup, 97
Smoked Sausage Stew, 95
Texas Queso Dip, 59
Shredded Pork, 177
Simple Salted Carrots, 189
Simply Apple Dump Cake, 243
Simply Delicious Chicken Breasts, 123
6-Can Soup, 105
Sloppy Joes, 159
Slow Cooked Honey Garlic Chicken
Thighs, 115
Slow-Cooked Swiss Steak, 142
Slow-Cooker Cheese Potatoes, 214
Slow-Cooker Chicken and Gravy, 127
Smoked Sausage Stew, 95
soup
Beef Barley Soup, 83

Broccoli Cheese Soup, 107
Buffalo Chicken Wing Soup, 71
Chili Taco Soup, 79
Chunky Chicken Vegetable Soup, 65
Cream of Broccoli Soup, 108
Easy Chicken Tortilla Soup, 69
Ground Beef Vegetable Soup, 81
Harry's Vegetable Soup, 102
Kelly's Split Pea Soup, 93
Kielbasa Soup, 97
Mary's Chicken and Rice Soup, 66
Mountain Bike Soup, 94
Quick Taco Chicken Soup, 67
Santa Fe Soup with Melted Cheese, 80
6-Can Soup, 105
Taco Soup, 77
Taco Soup with Pinto Beans, 78
Tasty Chicken Soup, 64
Tomato Vegetable Soup, 103
sour cream
Buffalo Chicken Wing Soup, 71
Cozy Cabin Casserole, 140
Easy Creamy Chicken, 122
Slow-Cooker Cheese Potatoes, 214
Southwest Hot Chip Dip, 55
Spiced Coffee, 265
Spiced Cranberry Cider, 273
Spicy French Dip, 147
Spicy Hot Cider, 271
Streusel Cake, 29
stuffing mix
Chicken and Stuffing, 130
Creamy Baked Chicken with Stuffing,
131
Sunday Chicken Dinner, 126
Super Beef Barbecue, 152

Sweet 'n Sour Meatballs, 49
sweet potatoes
    Barbecued Green Beans, 201
    Carolina Pot Roast, 169
Swiss Steak and Gravy, 141

T
Taco Soup, 77
Taco Soup with Pinto Beans, 78
Tapioca Salad, 259
Tasty Chicken Soup, 64
Tender Barbecued Chicken, 117
Tender Tasty Ribs, 173
Texas Queso Dip, 59
Tina's Cheese Dip, 57
tomatoes
    Beans and Tomato Chili, 109
    Chicken with Vegetables, 129
    Easy Chicken Tortilla Soup, 69
    Extra Easy Chili, 87
    Mary's Chicken and Rice Soup, 66
    Santa Fe Soup with Melted Cheese, 80
    6-Can Soup, 105
    Southwest Hot Chip Dip, 55
    Taco Soup with Pinto Beans, 78
    Texas Queso Dip, 59
tomato juice
    Ground Beef Vegetable Soup, 81
tomato sauce
    Chunky Chicken Vegetable Soup, 65
    Easy Chicken Tortilla Soup, 69
    Pizza Potatoes, 213
    Taco Soup with Pinto Beans, 78
    Versatile Slow-Cooker Chili, 90

tomato soup
    Hassle-Free Pork Chops, 167
    6-Can Soup, 105
    Taco Soup, 77
Tomato Vegetable Soup, 103
turkey
    Chunky Chicken Vegetable Soup, 65
    ground
        Easy Meatloaf, 153
        Extra Easy Chili, 87
        Turkey Chili, 73
        Versatile Slow-Cooker Chili, 90
Turkey Chili, 73

V
vanilla pudding
    Funfetti Dump Cake, 239
Velveeta
    Chili-Cheese Taco Dip, 56
    Layered Breakfast Casserole, 16
    Santa Fe Soup with Melted Cheese, 80
    Southwest Hot Chip Dip, 55
    Texas Queso Dip, 59
Versatile Slow-Cooker Chili, 90

W
Whole Dinner Roast Beef, 139

Y
yogurt
    Greek Chicken Pita Filling, 121

Z
Zesty French Dip, 143

About the Author

Hope Comerford is a mom, wife, elementary music teacher, blogger, recipe developer, public speaker, ALM Zone fit leader, Young Living Essential Oils essential oil enthusiast/educator, and published author. In 2013, she was diagnosed with a severe gluten intolerance and since then has spent many hours creating easy, practical, and delicious gluten-free recipes that can be enjoyed by both those who are affected by gluten and those who are not.

Growing up, Hope spent many hours in the kitchen with her Meme (grandmother) and her love for cooking grew from there. While working on her master's degree when her daughter was young, Hope turned to her slow cookers for some salvation and sanity. It was from there she began truly experimenting with recipes and quickly learned she had the ability to get a little more creative in the kitchen and develop her own recipes.

In 2010, Hope started her blog, *A Busy Mom's Slow Cooker Adventures*, to simply share the recipes she was making with her family and friends. She never imagined people all over the world would begin visiting her page and sharing her recipes with others as well. In 2013, Hope self-published her first cookbook, *Slow Cooker Recipes 10 Ingredients or Less and Gluten-Free*, and then later wrote *The Gluten-Free Slow Cooker*.

Hope became the new brand ambassador and author of Fix-It and Forget-It in mid-2016. Since then, she has brought her excitement and creativeness to the Fix-It and Forget-It brand. Through Fix-It and Forget-It, she has written *Fix-It and Forget-It Lazy & Slow, Fix-It and Forget-It Healthy Slow Cooker Cookbook, Fix-It and Forget-It Cooking for Two, Fix-It and Forget-It Instant Pot Cookbook, Fix-It and Forget-It Freezer Meals, Fix-It and Forget-It Healthy 5-Ingredient Cookbook, Fix-It and Forget-It Keto Comfort Foods*, and more.

Hope lives in the city of Clinton Township, Michigan, near Metro Detroit. She has been happily married to her husband and best friend, Justin, since 2008. Together they have two children, Ella and Gavin, who are her motivation, inspiration, and heart. In her spare time, Hope enjoys traveling, singing, cooking, reading books, spending time with friends and family, and relaxing.